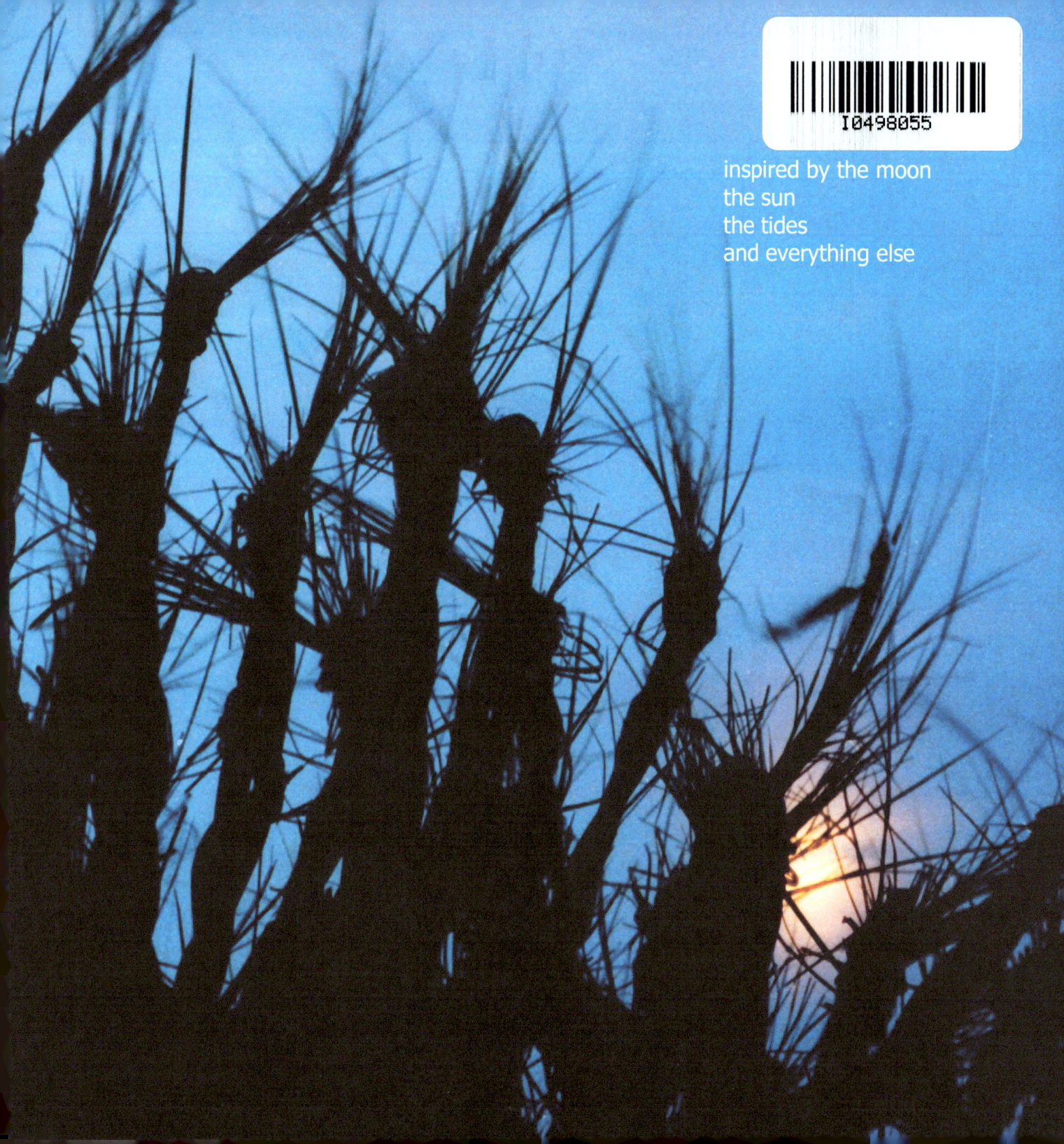

inspired by the moon
the sun
the tides
and everything else

64 Tufts

At the top of the big sand dune at Saunton Burrows I plaited the long sharp grass ready for moon rise.

My hands were well spiky after.

Martin and I played body boarding down the dune until dark.

Later we listened to night noises and ate supper in the moon light.

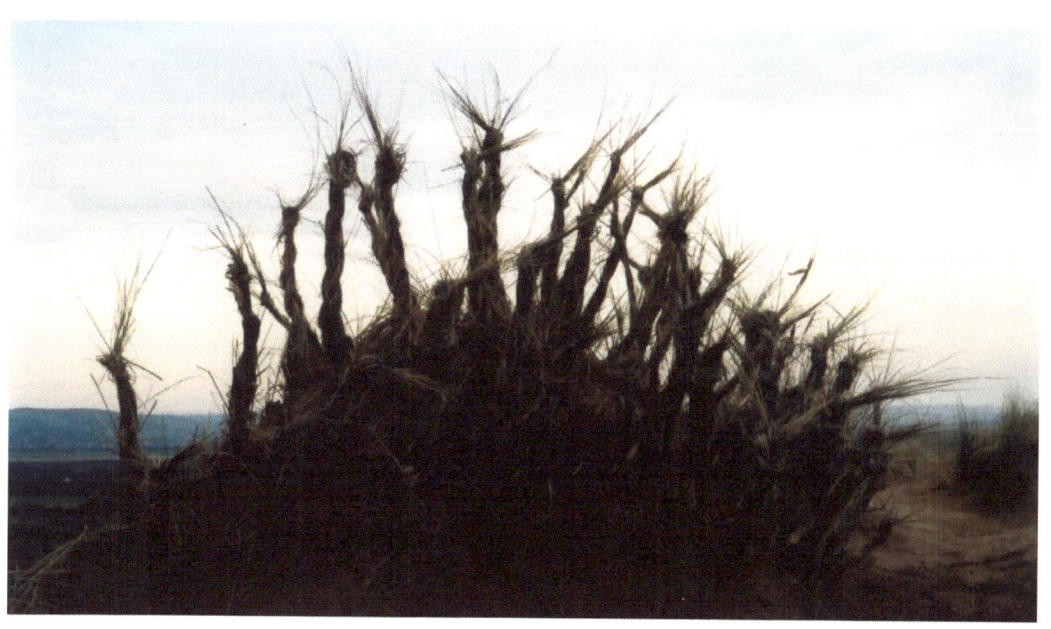
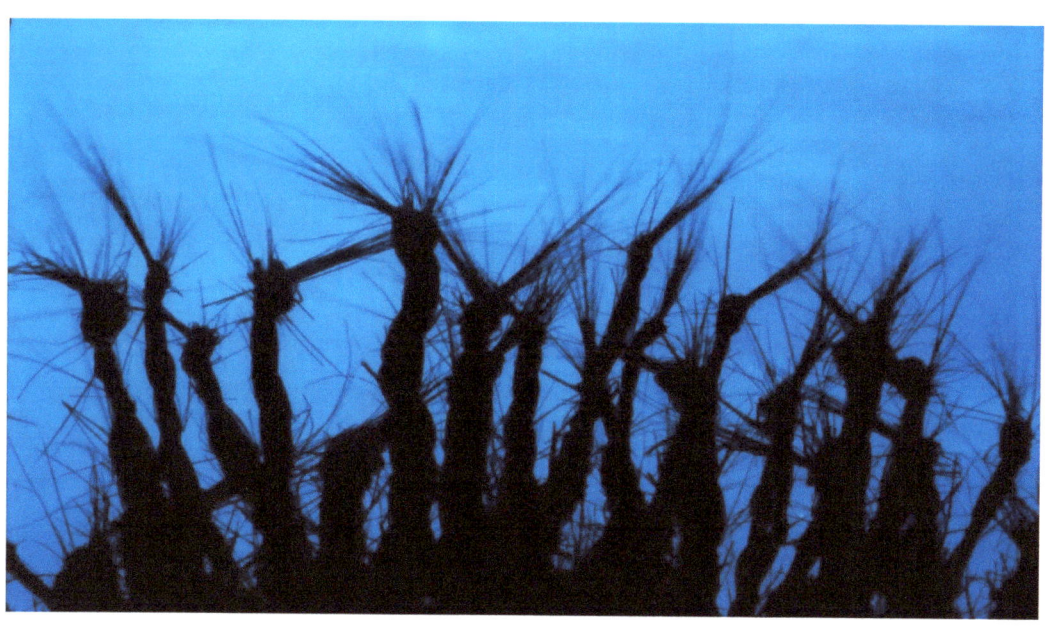

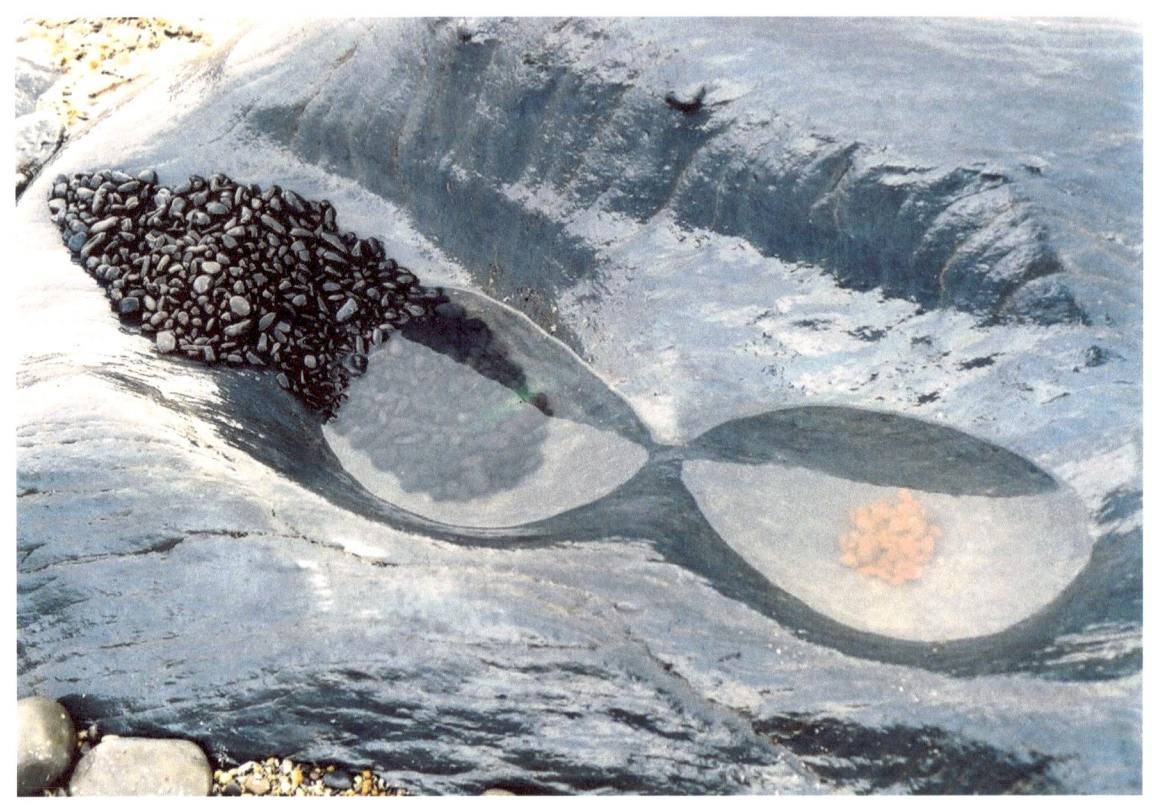

Raining and no one about – brilliant!

I store some of my collections in secret places about the beach.

I brought these black pebbles out of hiding and left them for the tide.

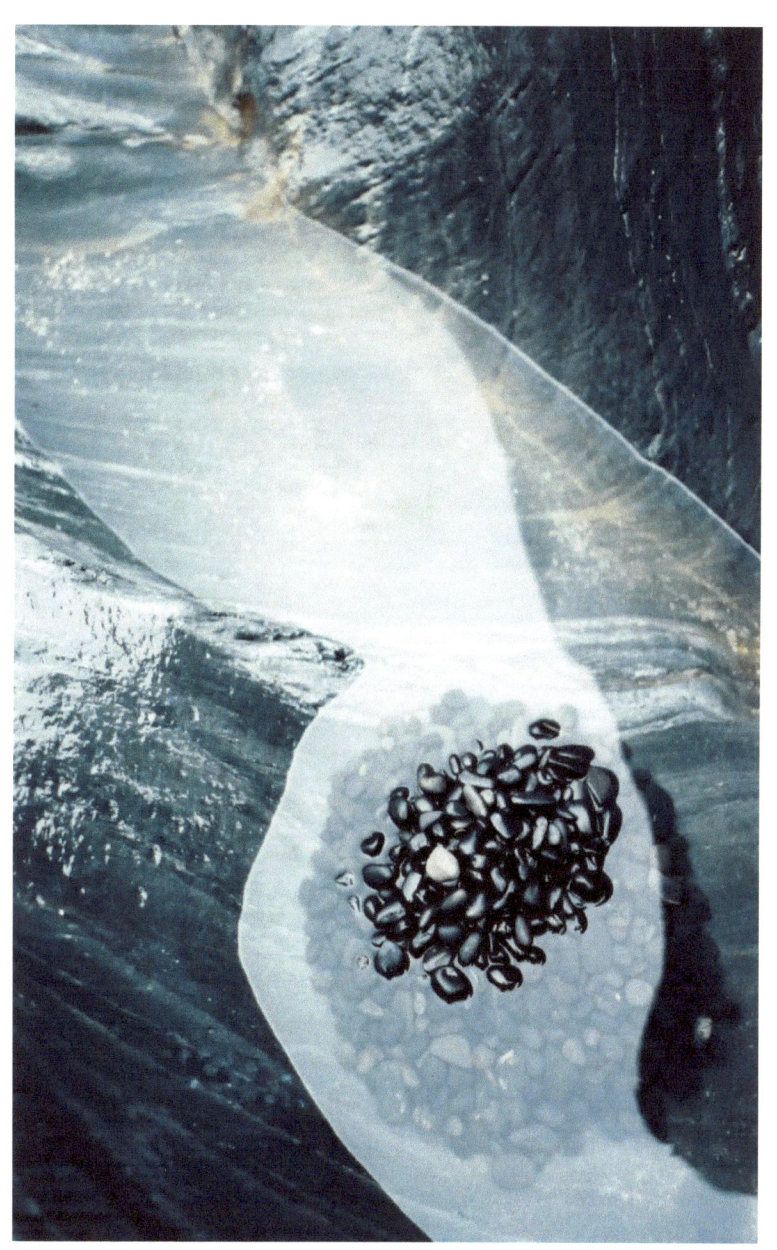

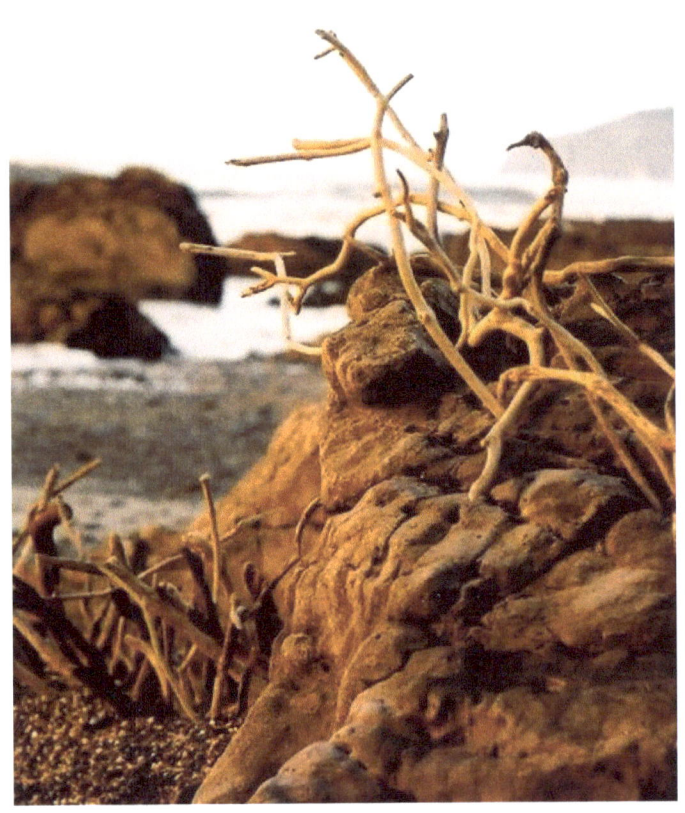

Martin and I had spent a few days creating whilst the moon was at its fullest – of course he knew all the times of rises and set.

But on this day, this particular day, it was just beautiful I didn't give the moon a second thought, it was obviously doing its orbital thing regardless.

Anyway, we arrived at Down End beach late afternoon, it was a rush to get all the driftwood in place before the tide came in. We stayed until the sun went down.

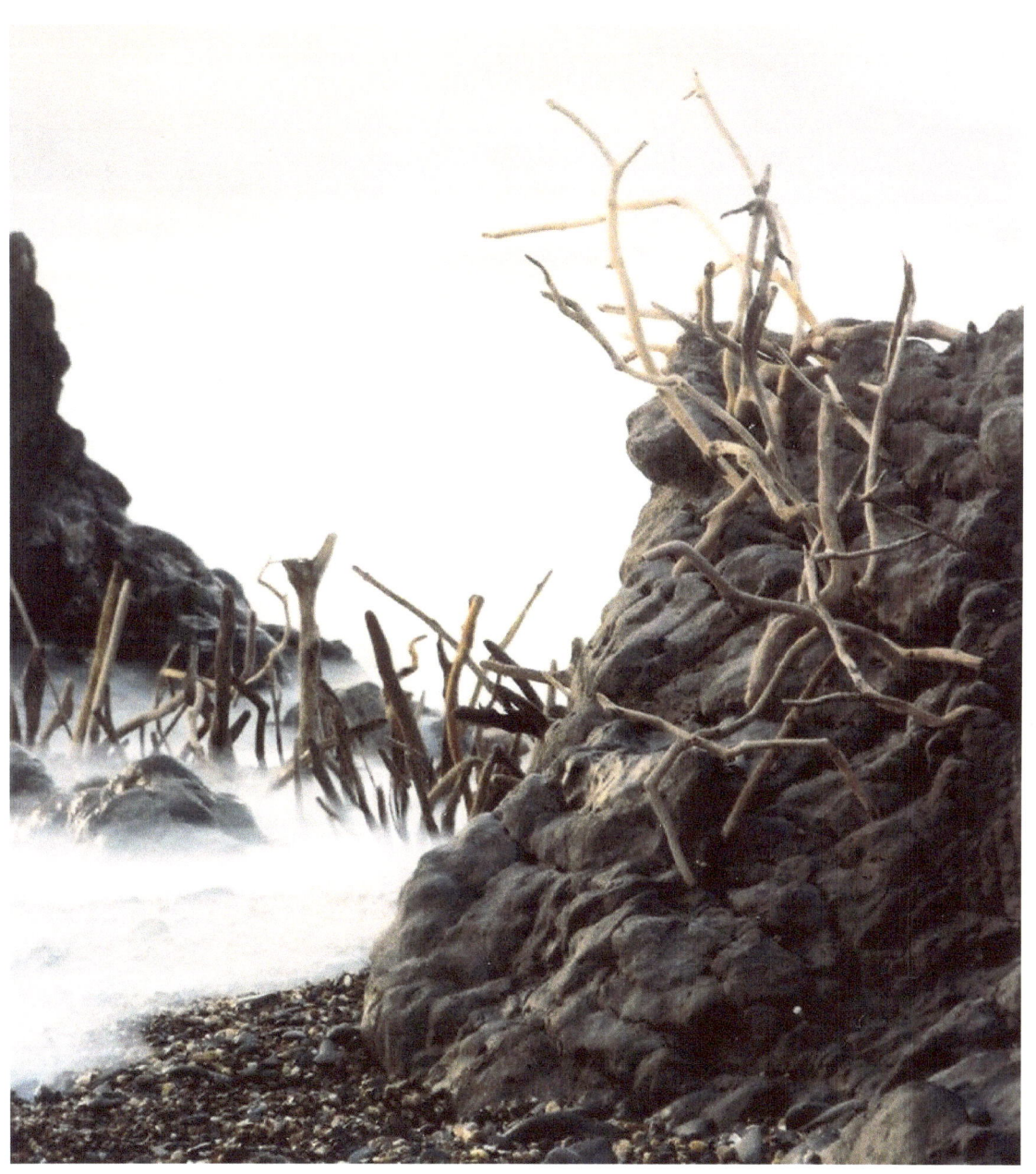

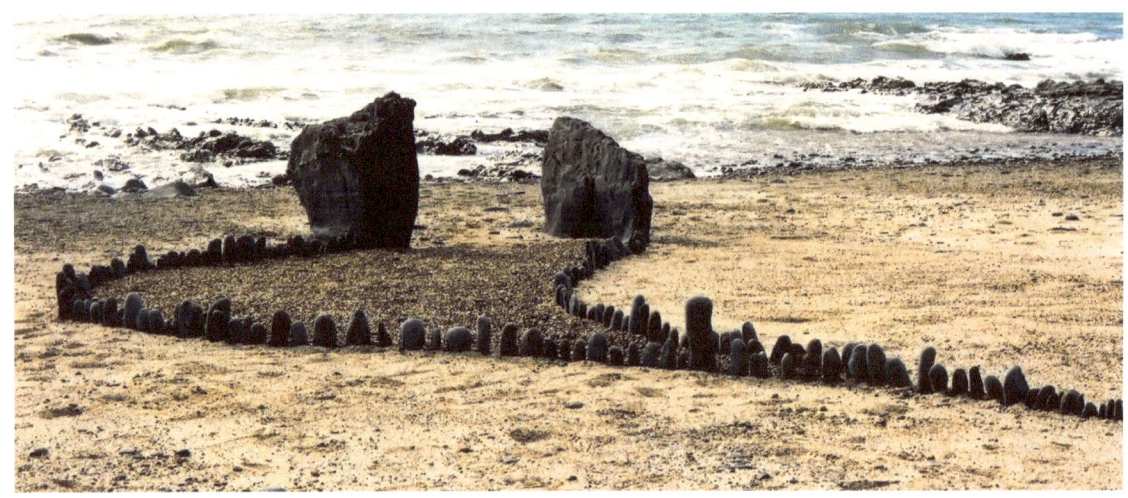

Above. I call the two tall rocks the teeth stones.

Below. Balancing stones is easier than you think once you get the gist

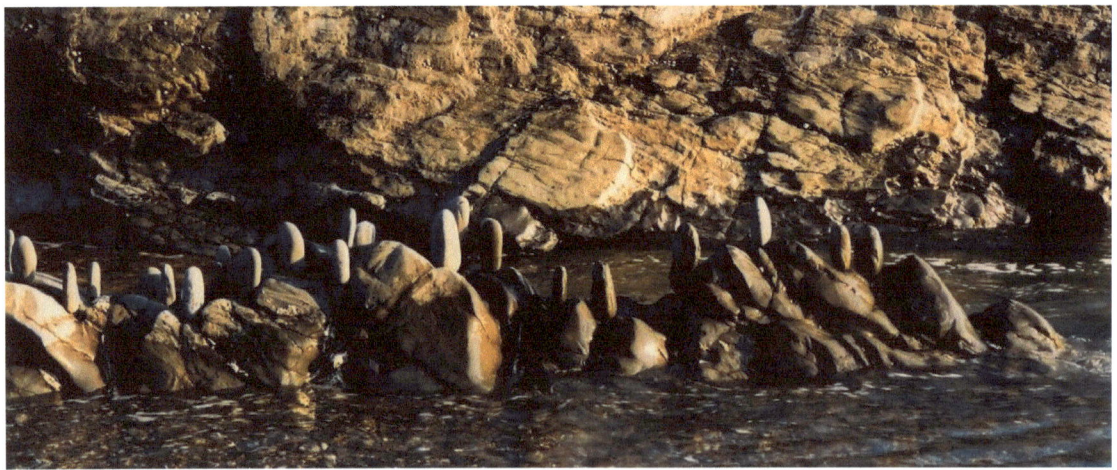

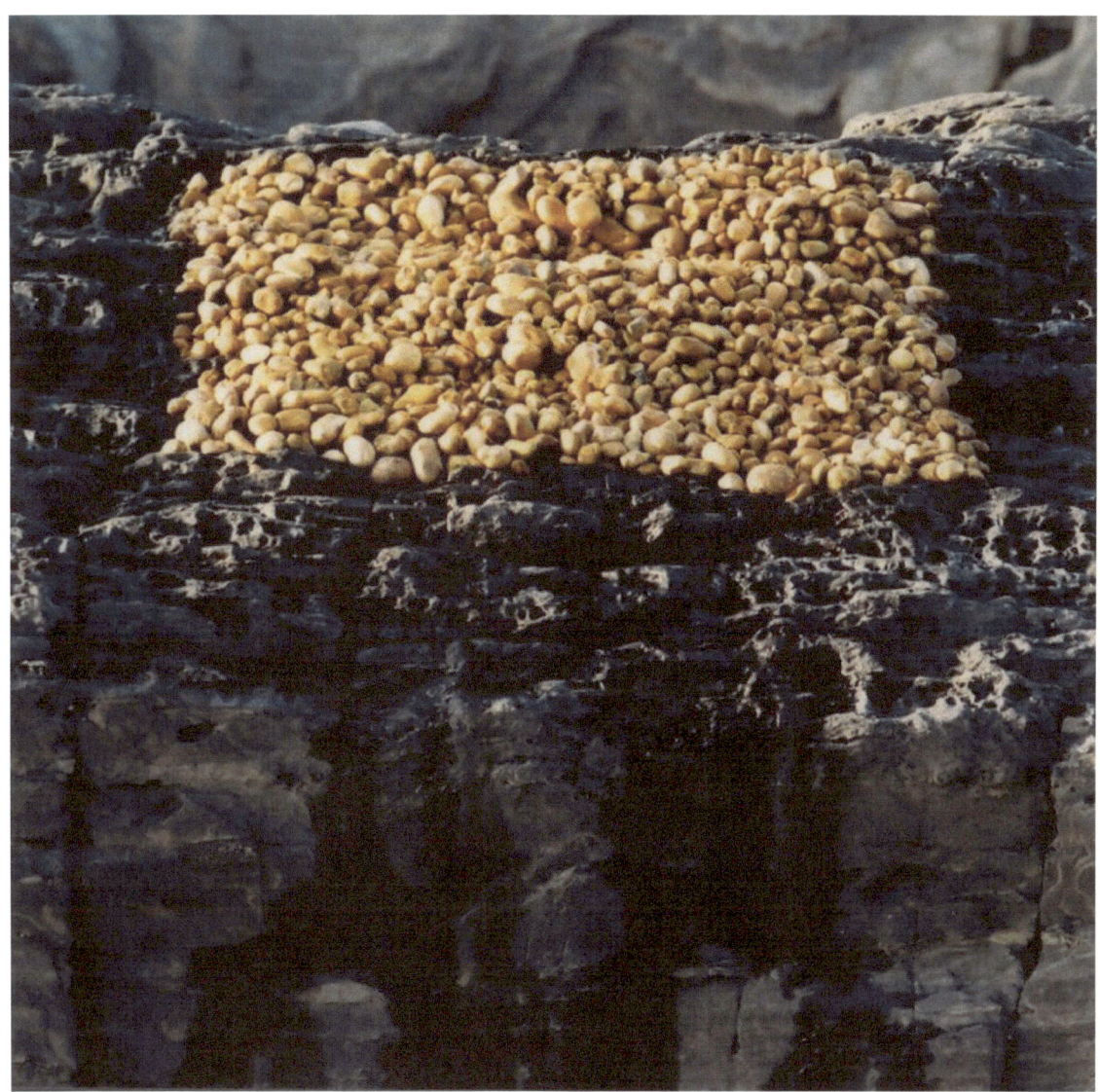

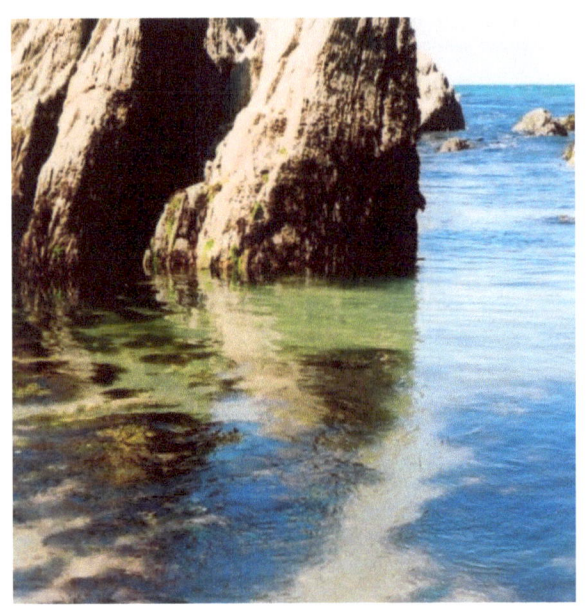

The tide blocks your escape if you don't watch it at Pensport Rock.

The sun shone all day Nathan and Hayley were fantastic glamorous assistants.

After construction was complete we dangled out feet in the water while we ate our picnic.

The pictures only give a tiny glimpse, but the memory of that day is treasure.

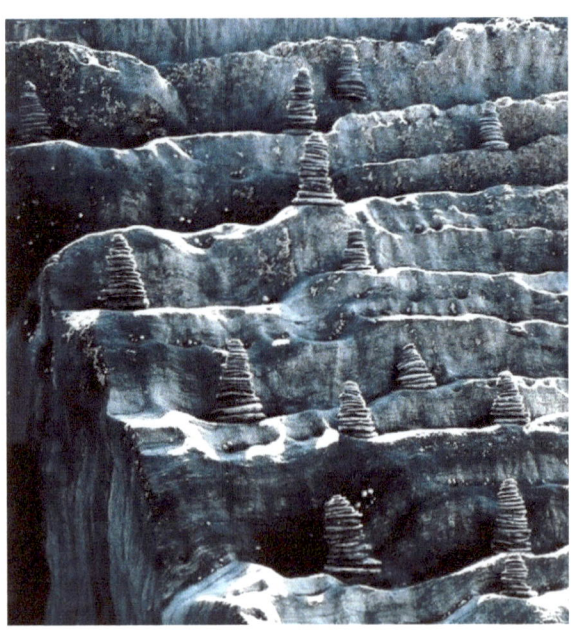
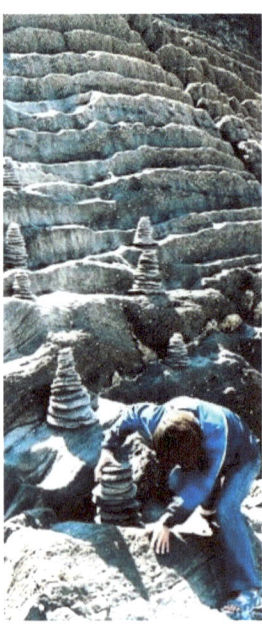
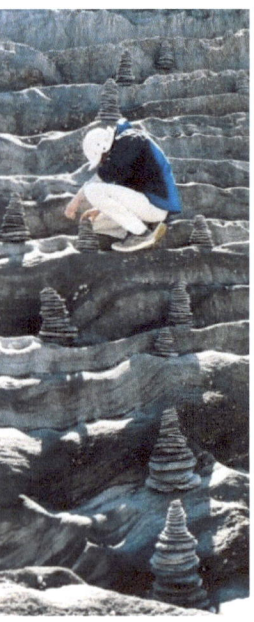

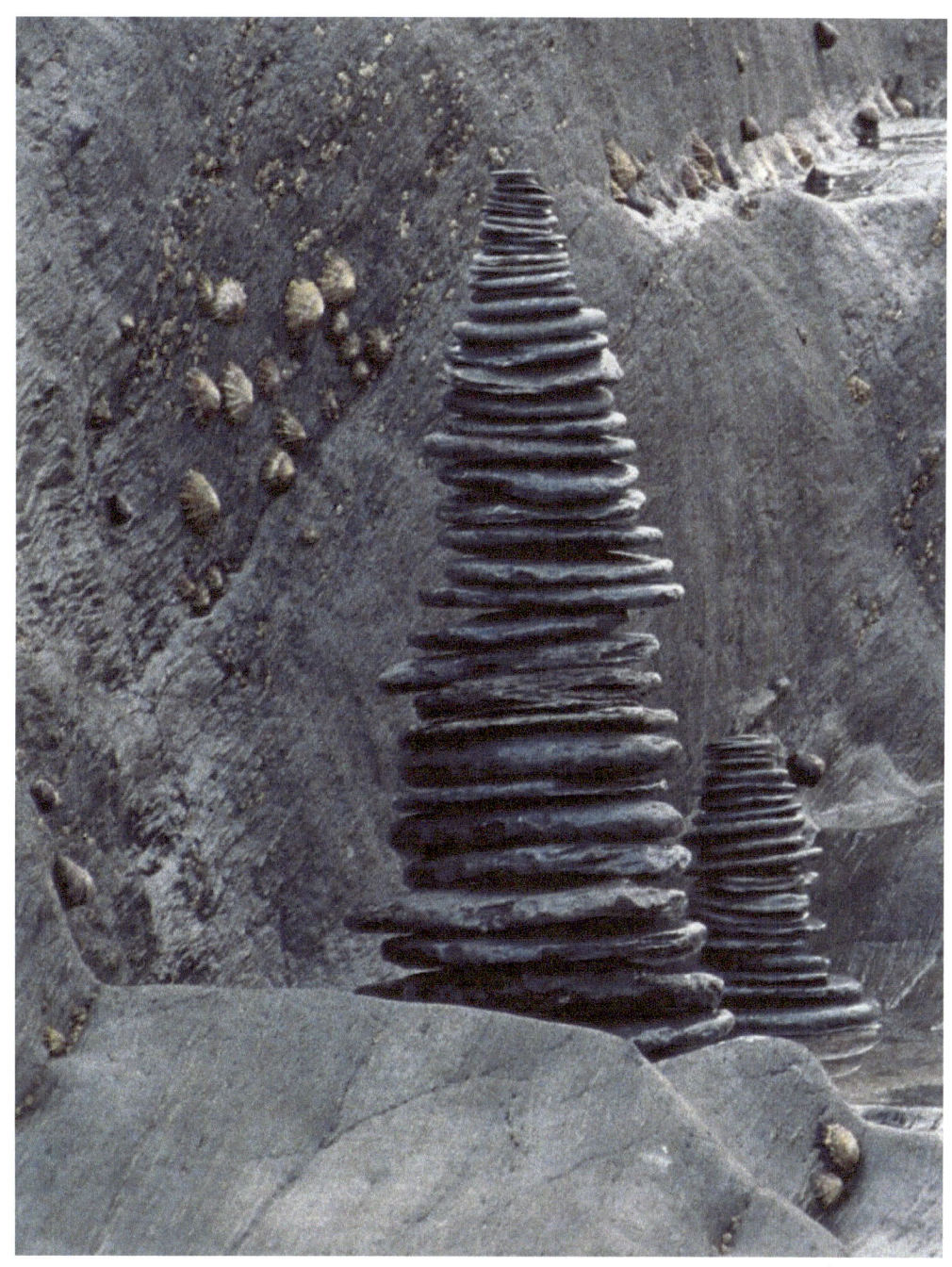

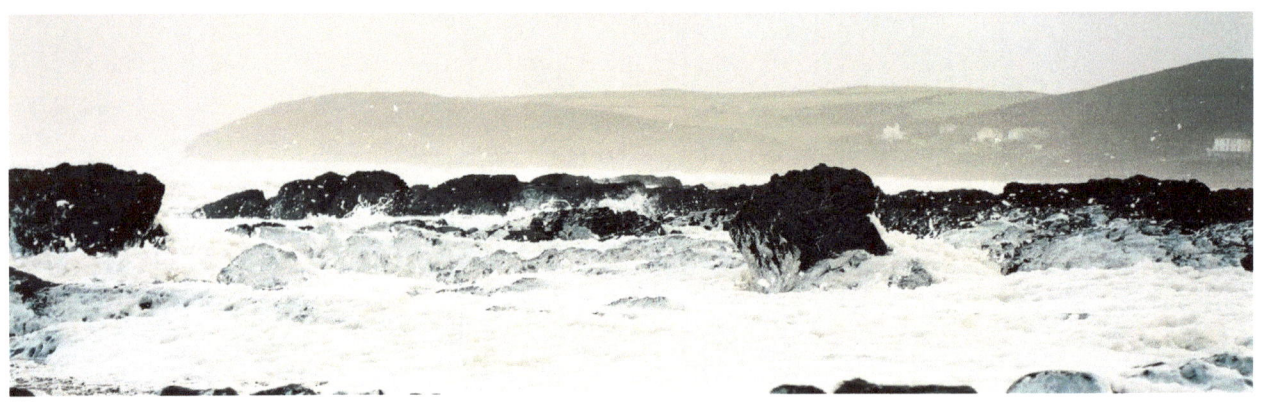

Down end beach catches the wind and keeps it swirling about just because it can.

To take the above photo I had to wedge myself between the rocks. I got covered in foam. It was great – although it took me ages to climb back to the path.

So…

I thought I would wait for a calm day for the feathers; I had collected them over time from local beaches and as you might expect - when I got there it was windy – incredibly windy and not calm at all and I had brought all the gear.

Neither hell nor high water was going to stop my creative flow, of course the feathers kept escaping and flying over the beach.

I ran about like a startled gazelle and laughed out loud. Only a few photos were useable – so don't be fooled by this illusion of stillness.

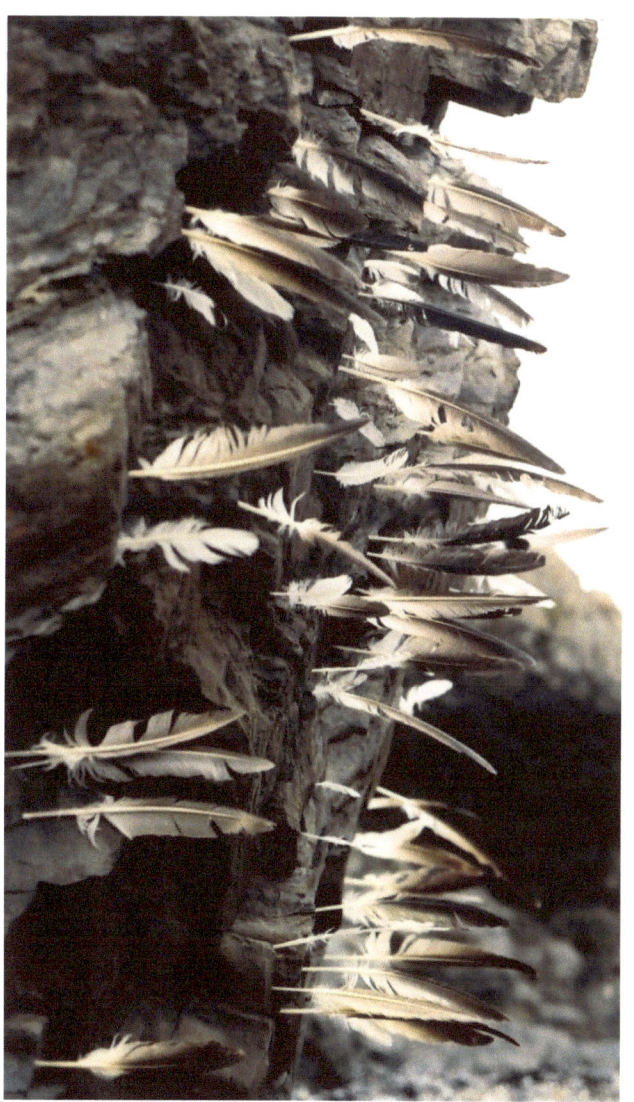

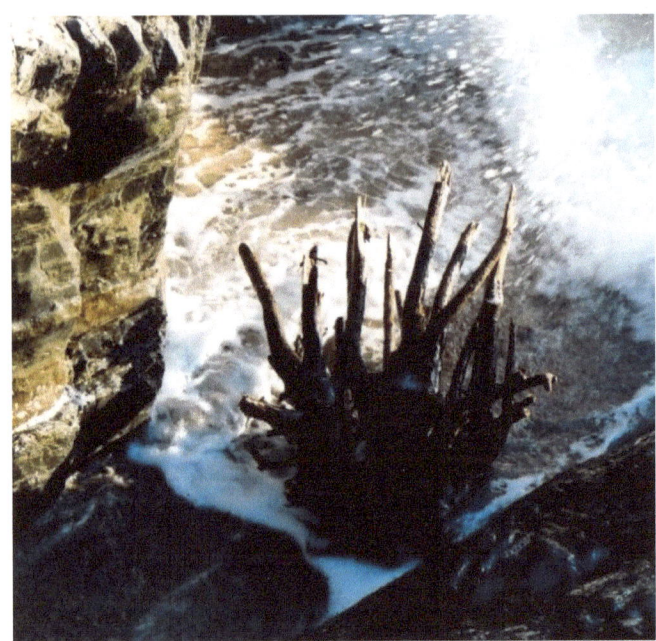

I could hear odd sounds so climbing up I wedged my feet - already wet of course against either side of the rocks. There I watched what looked like a huge creature of the deep coming ashore.

It was a monster root ball.

Well. I just had to make one!

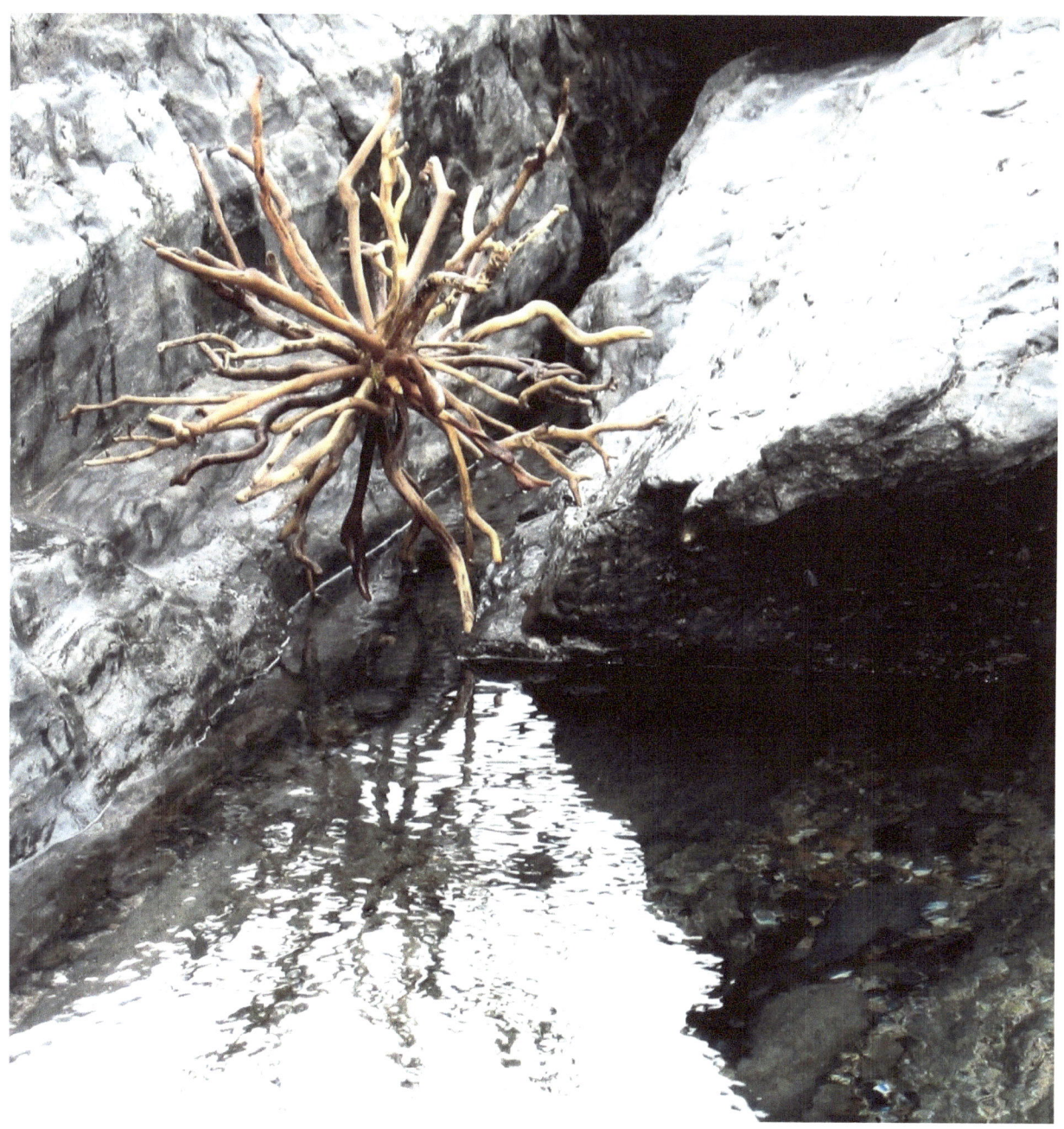

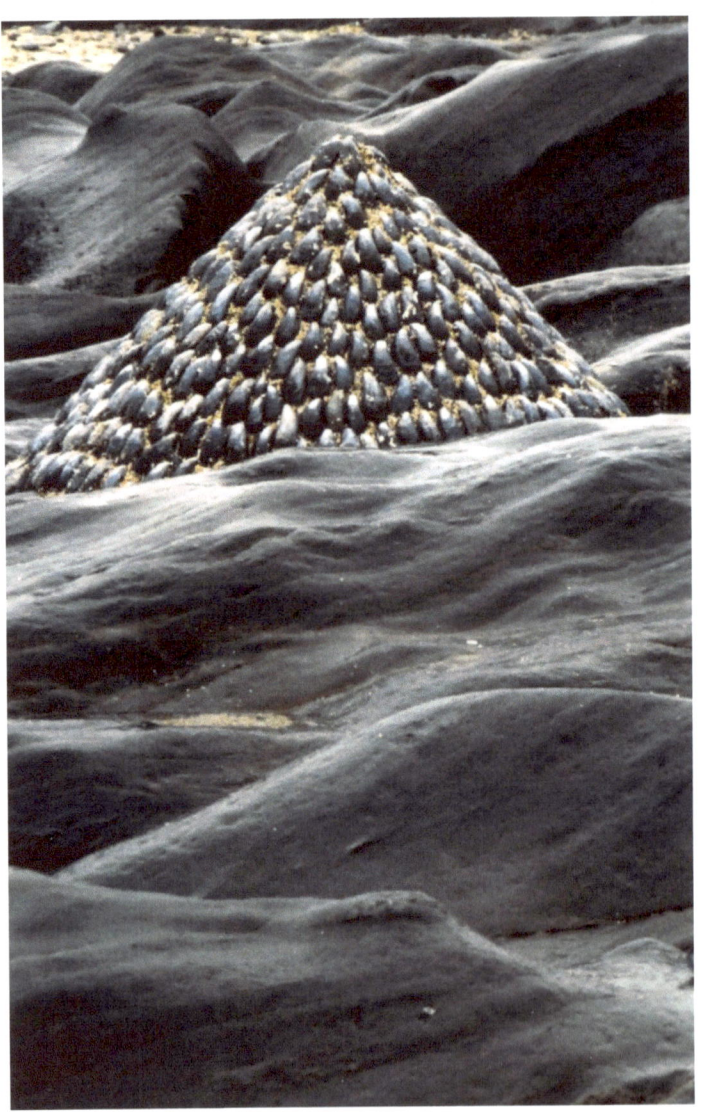

February - freezing cold thigh high in a rockpool.

I was on a mission. I knew the best place would be here on the base of the tooth stones.

They are only exposed now and then.

It took me hours it was nearly dark when I left.

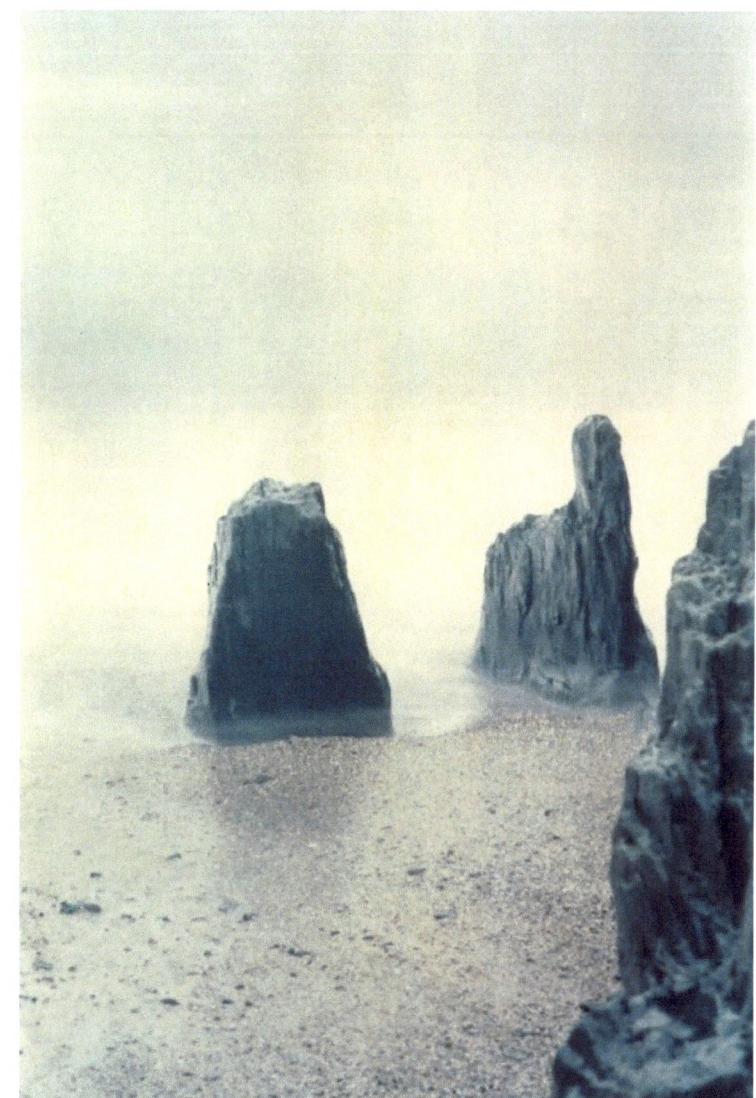

...reminds me of being there.

It was early, the incoming tide was quiet.

The mist deadened the sound even the seagulls seemed far away.

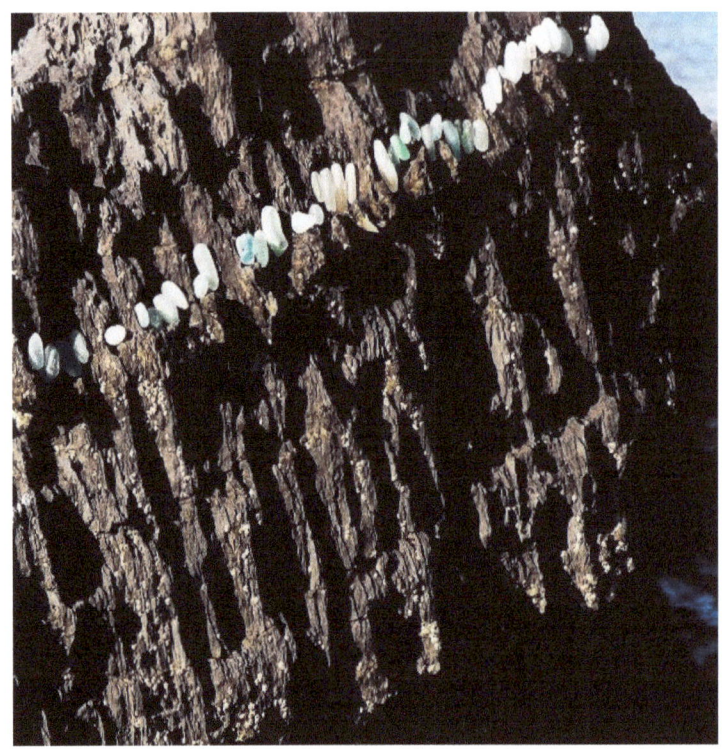

A bit of a climb this day but as the bright sunlight shone through the sea glass it was worth it.

Difficult to photograph though.

I have a jar full – I only keep the best bits.

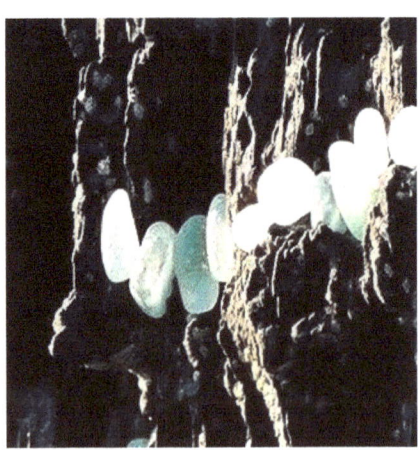

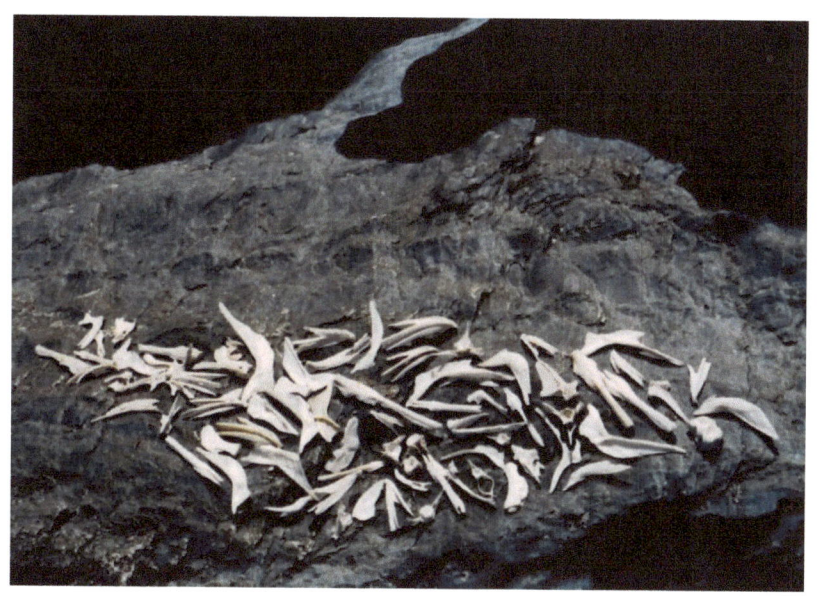

I don't normally go for bones, but I kept seeing them. So delicate that even the slightest breeze moved them as I tried to arrange them on the rock.

I took one home to keep.

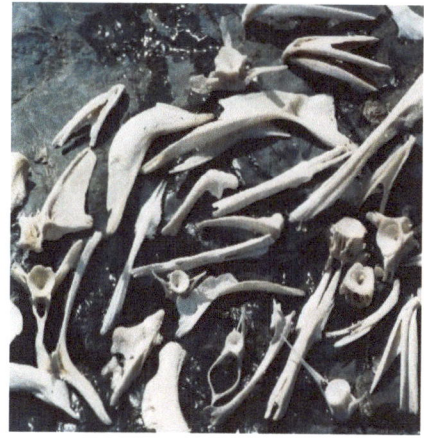

Nearly Autumn

Oyster catchers carried on doing their thing they took no notice of me making mud pies along the Braunton Estuary. Totally covered in mud I walked to crow point and ate my butties in the long grass.

On the way back, I had to face the fact that my sculpture looked remarkably like Dinosaur poo. Not that I have any knowledge of the bowel movements of Dinosaurs you understand – nor do I know any such creatures personally.

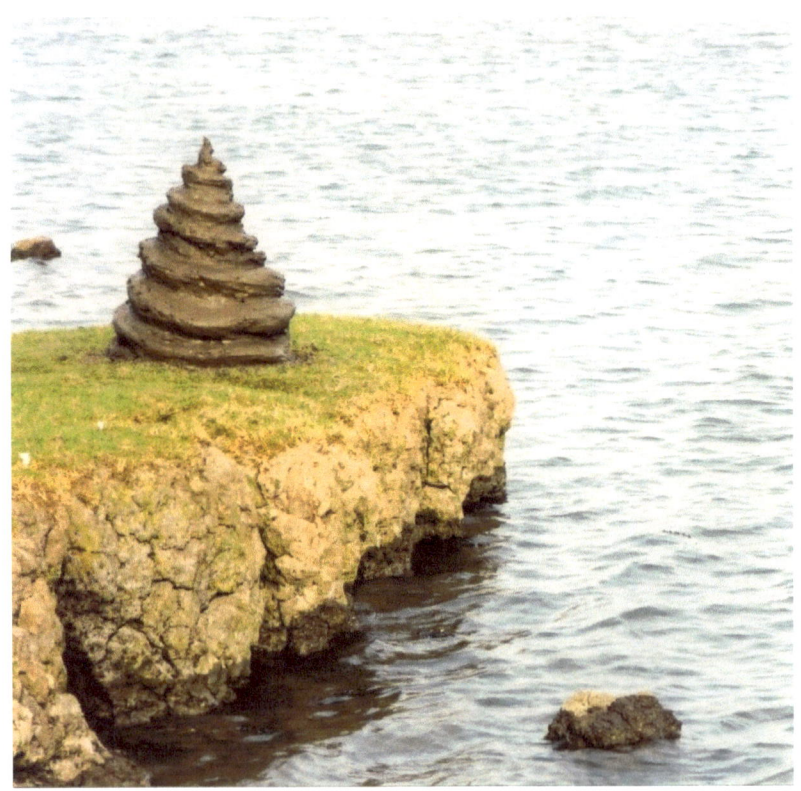

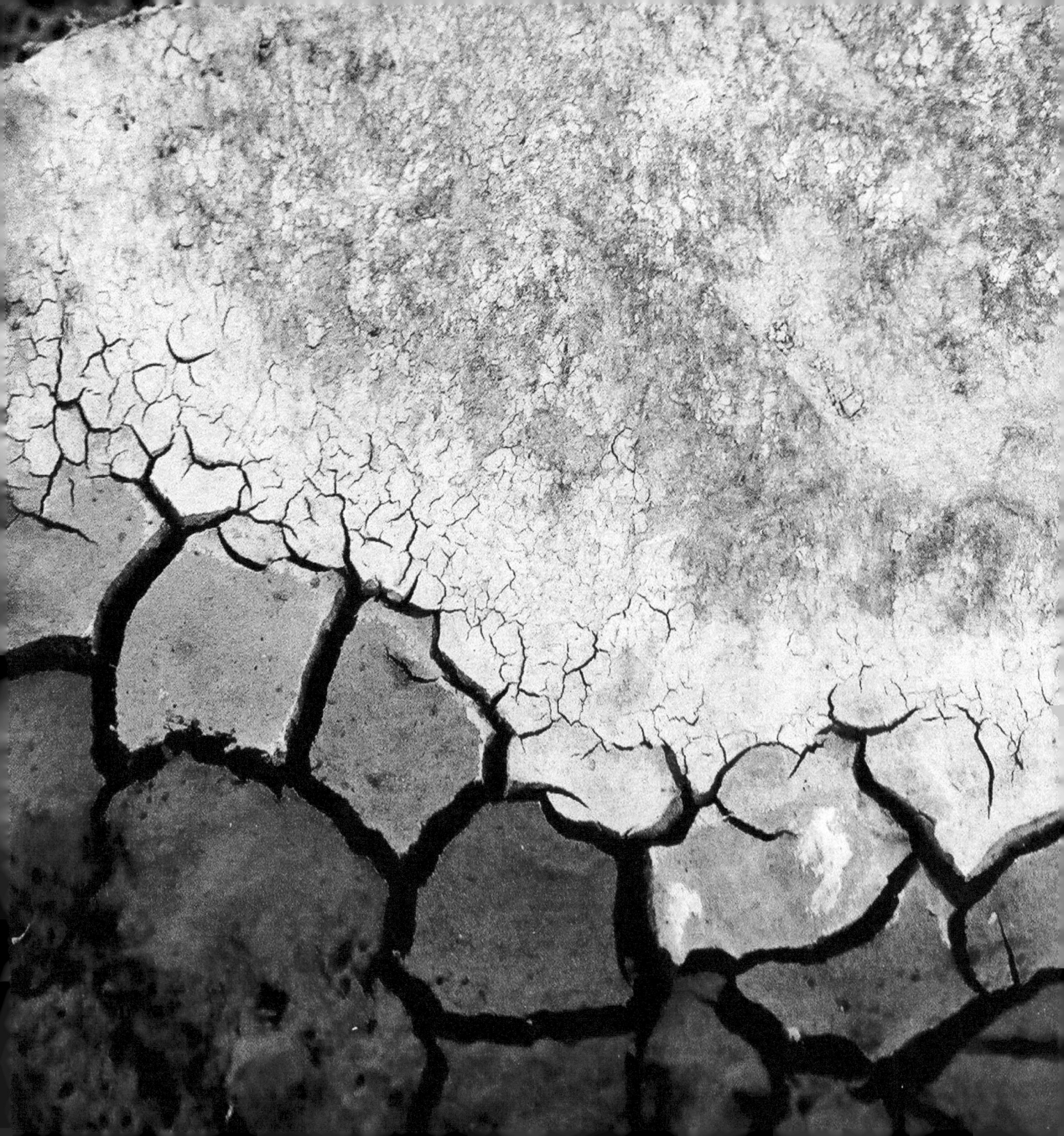

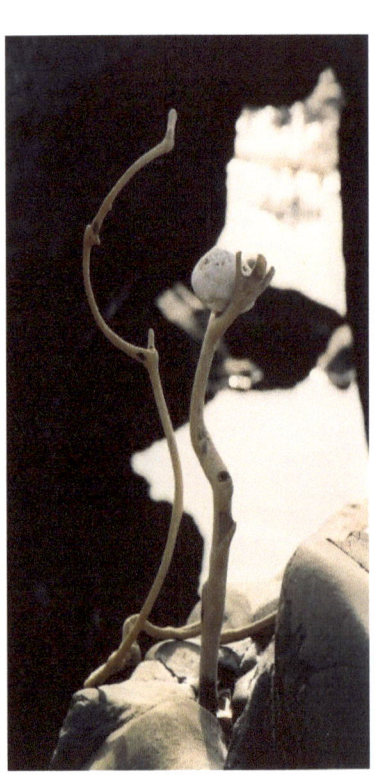 

It was hot, and the sea was flat.

Further down from my usual haunts there are hidden places where I go to be quiet.

I could see the sticks mirrored in the far pool – how to get there though hum?

Felt like I was climbing K2!

Although I do admit that to my knowledge there are no very large mountains by my house - but there are large sand dunes.

In any event it was a difficult climb over very big rocks.

I stayed for a while contemplating the return journey and watched the reflections.

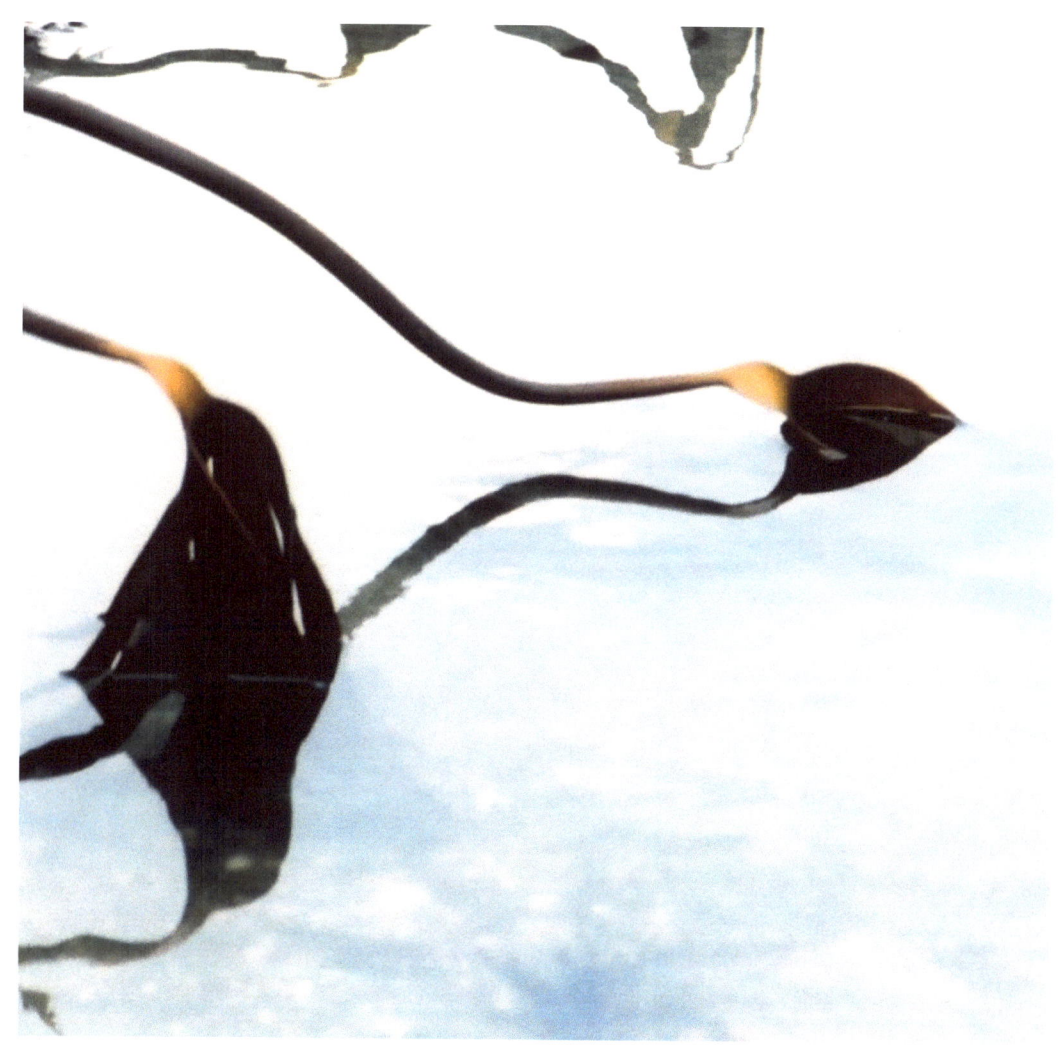

All these ideas evolved into an installation.

It took a while.

The exhibition was held In
'The Undertakers workshop'
Barnstaple Devon

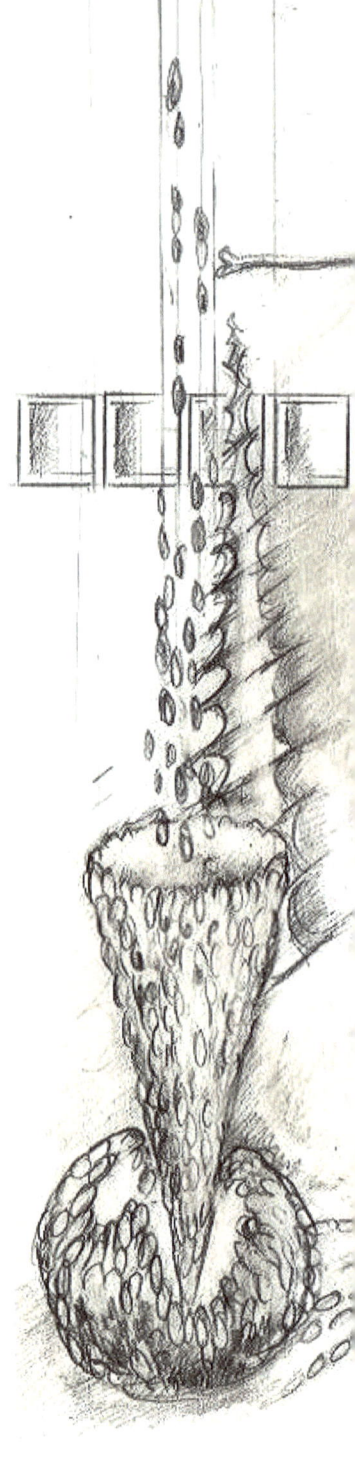

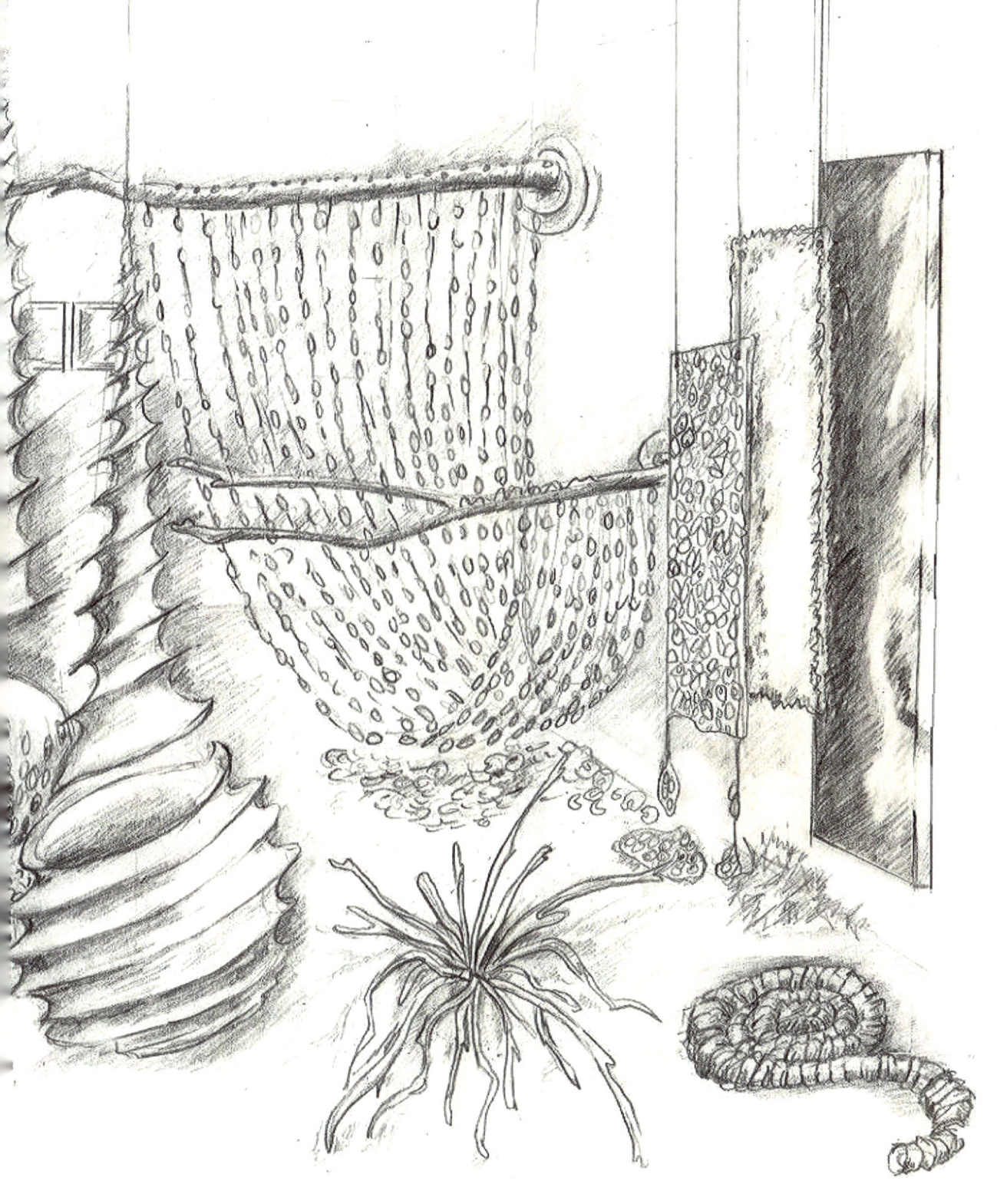

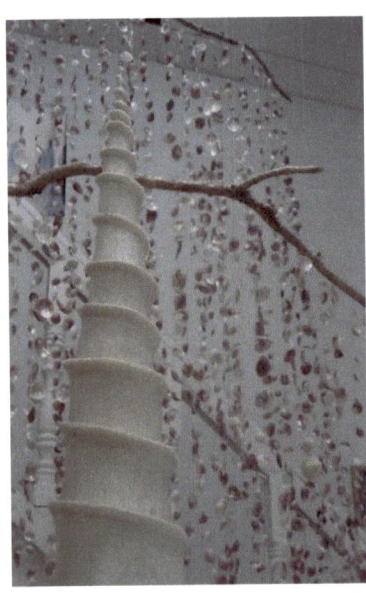

The installation was installed in the foyer.

We painted the whole area white before we set up as a surprising contrast to the colourful exhibition upstairs.

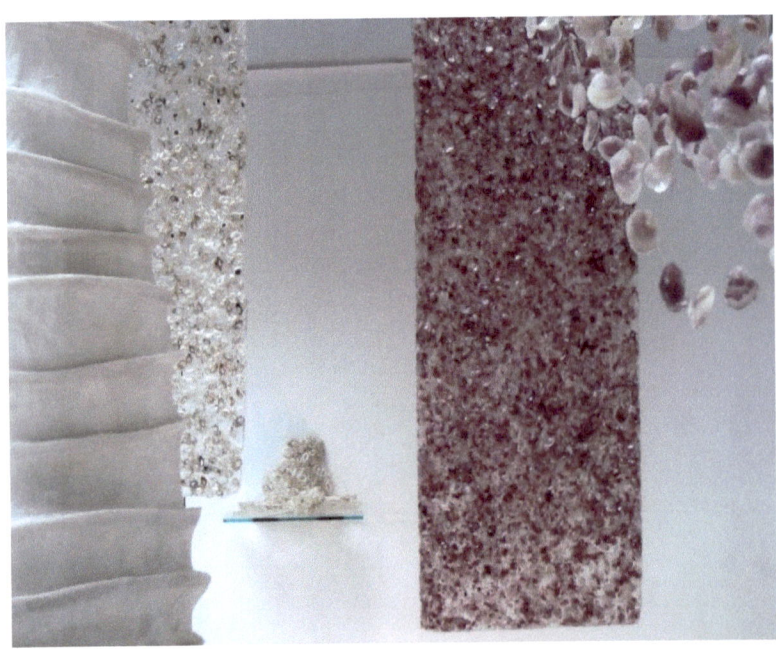

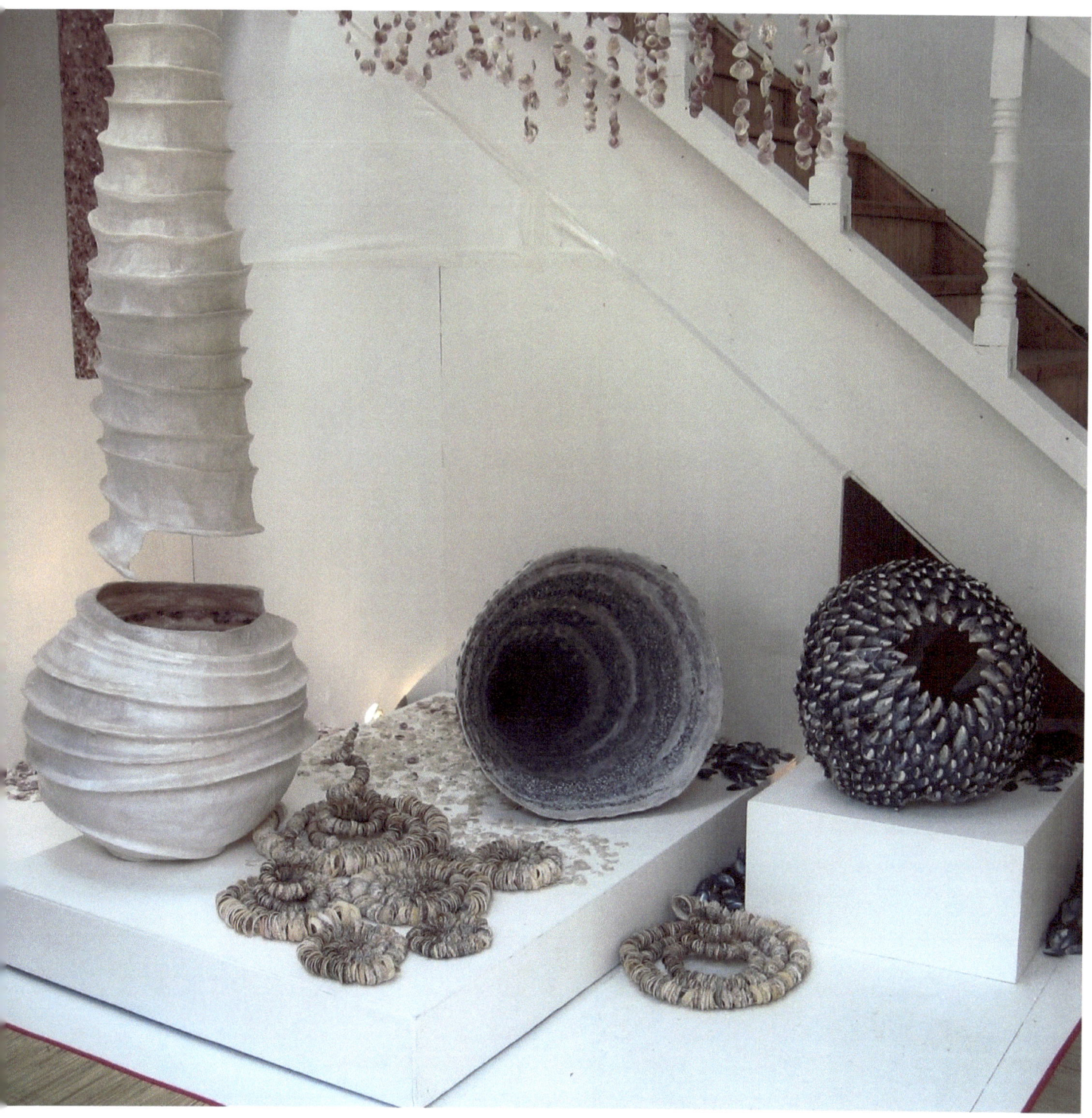

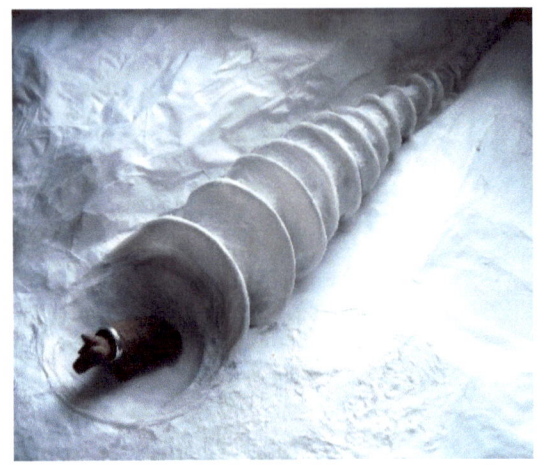

The original idea for these spiral drawings was for a large outdoor sculpture built in a dip suggesting a giant fossil housing a seated area and shallow pool.

Bottom right shows the seating area with drainage.

The shallow pool would be replenished by the rain. The whole would be a huge play area.

Modelled beautifully by Shep my nodding dog. Thank you Shep

Playing in sand

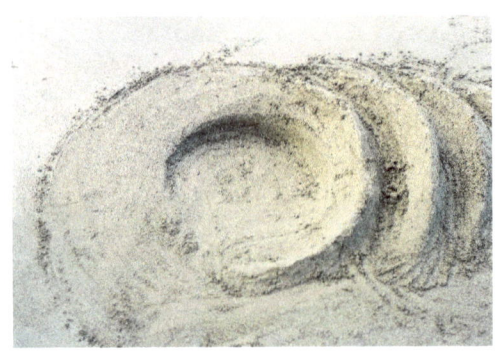

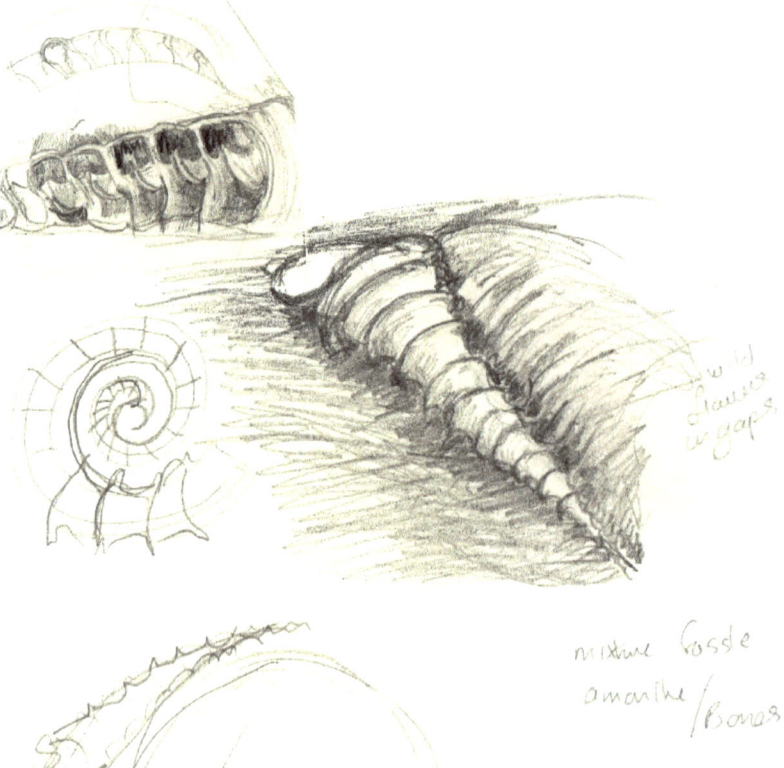

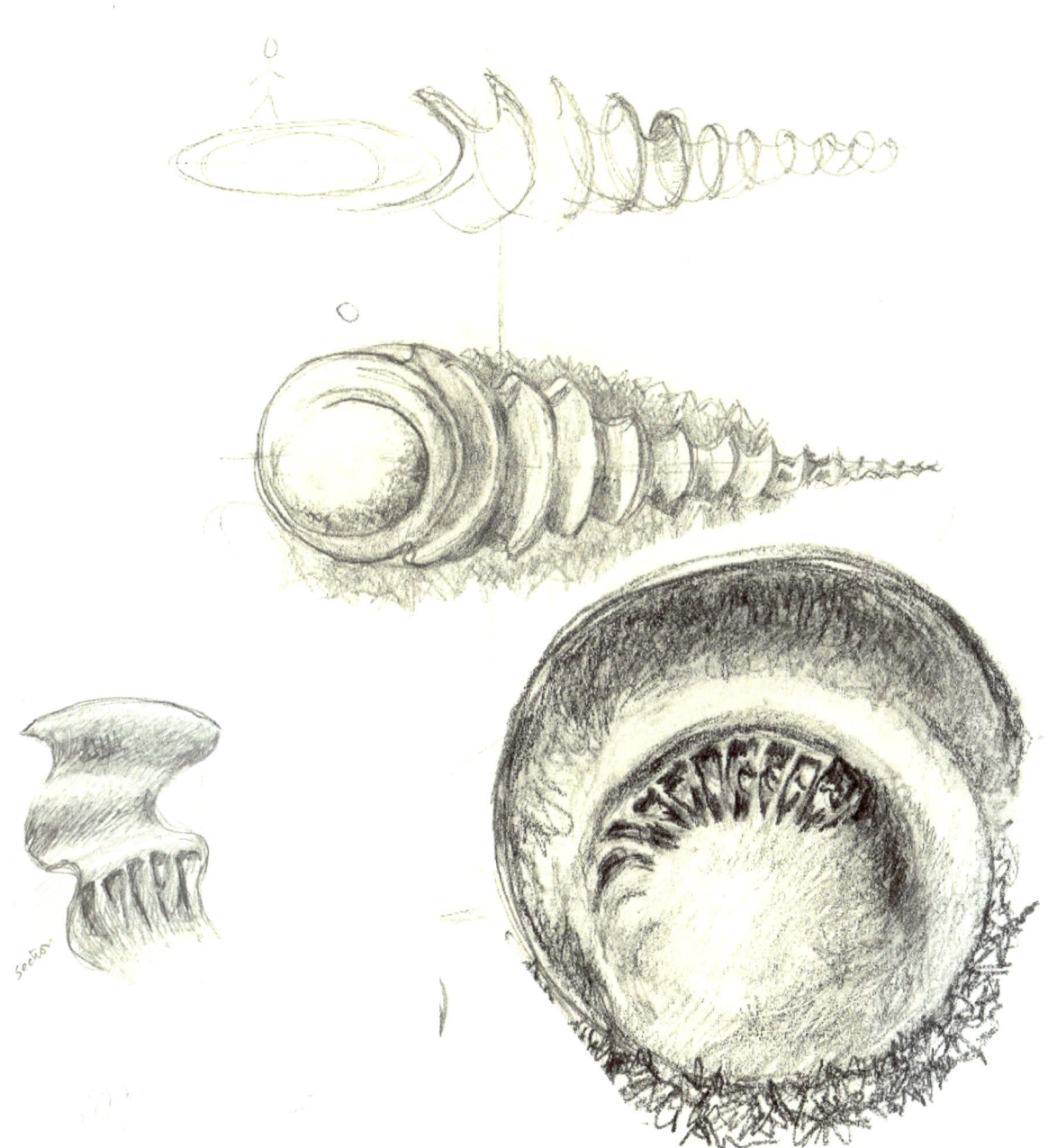

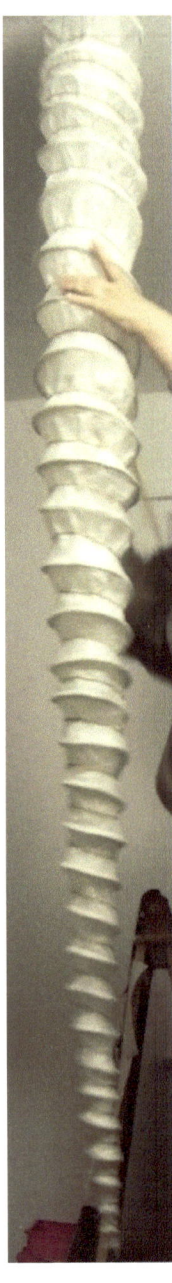

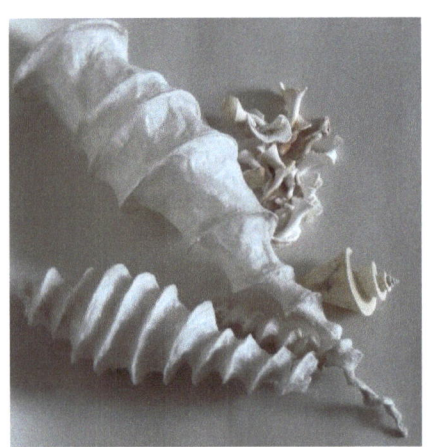

I enjoyed experimenting with the sculptural pieces amalgamating the various array of beach finds together with copious amounts of glue.

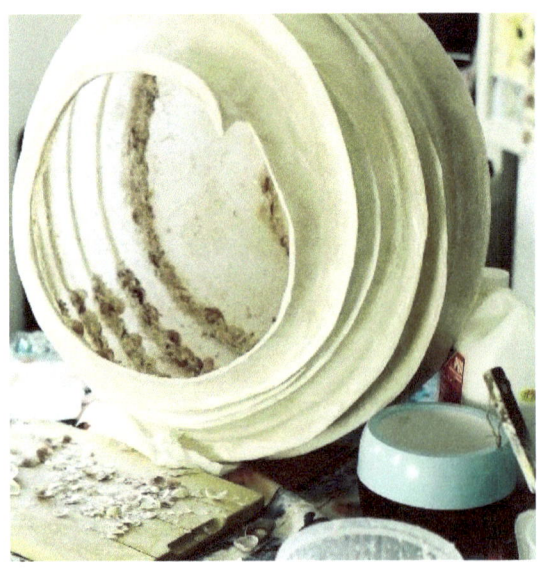

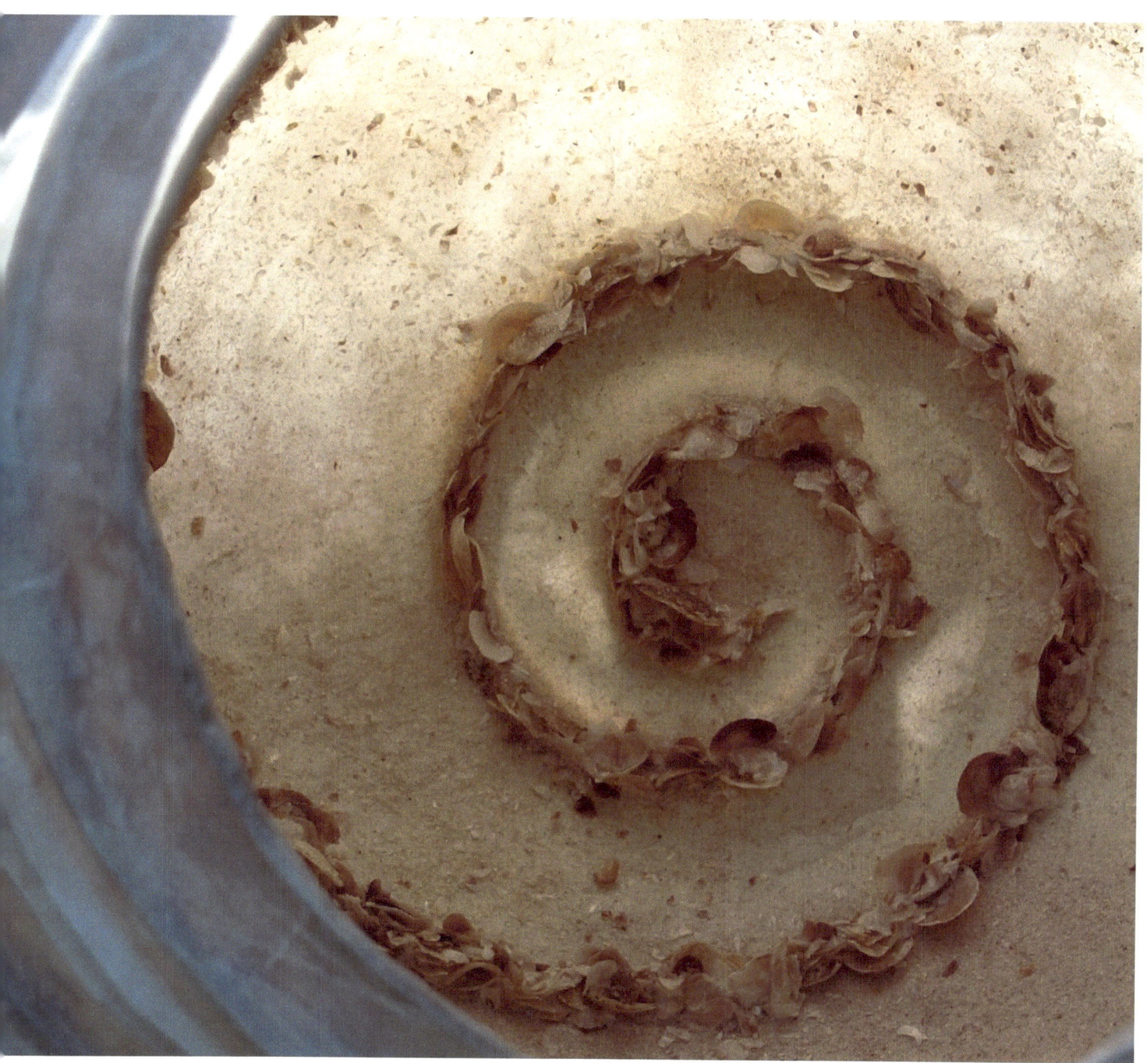

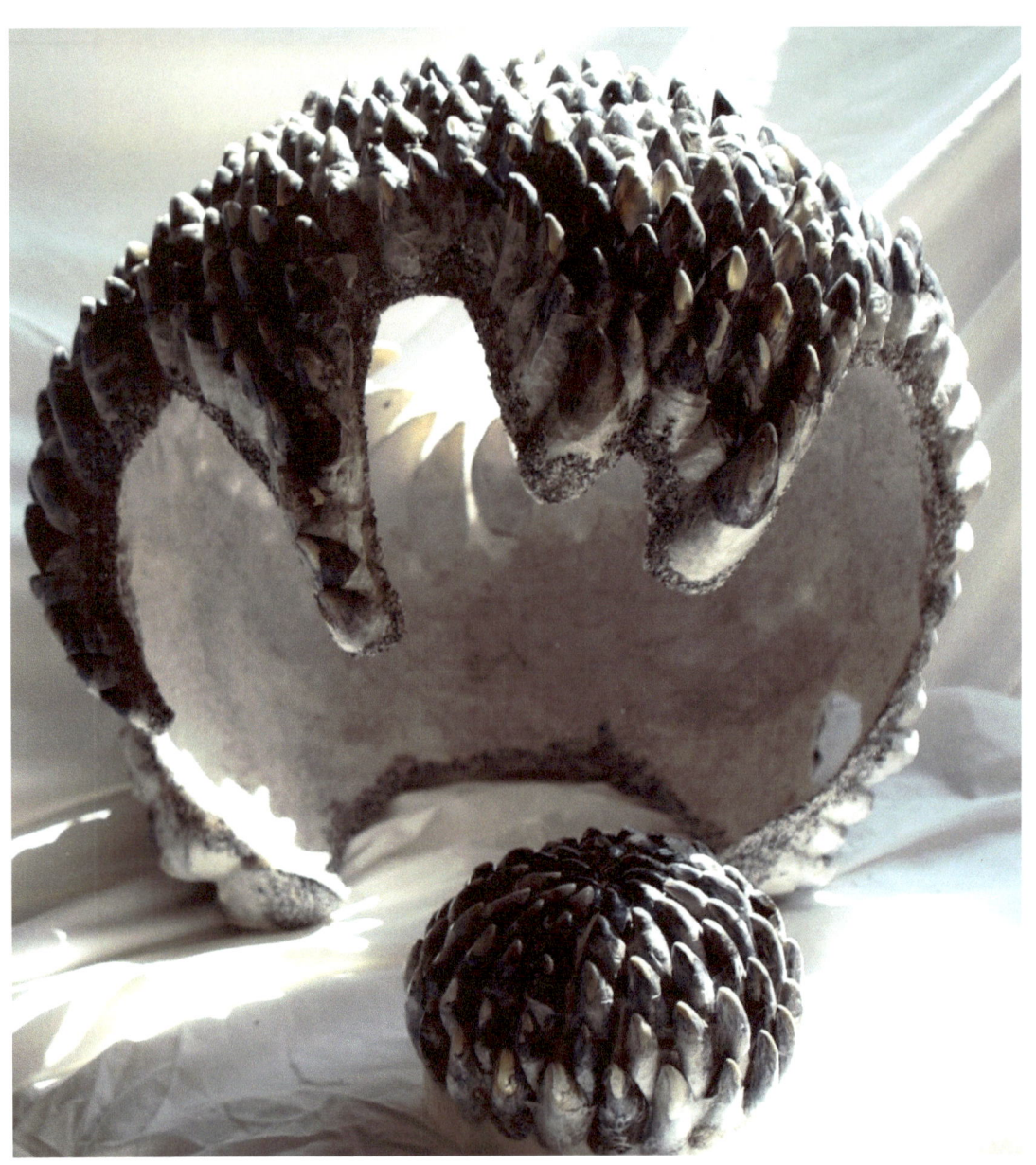

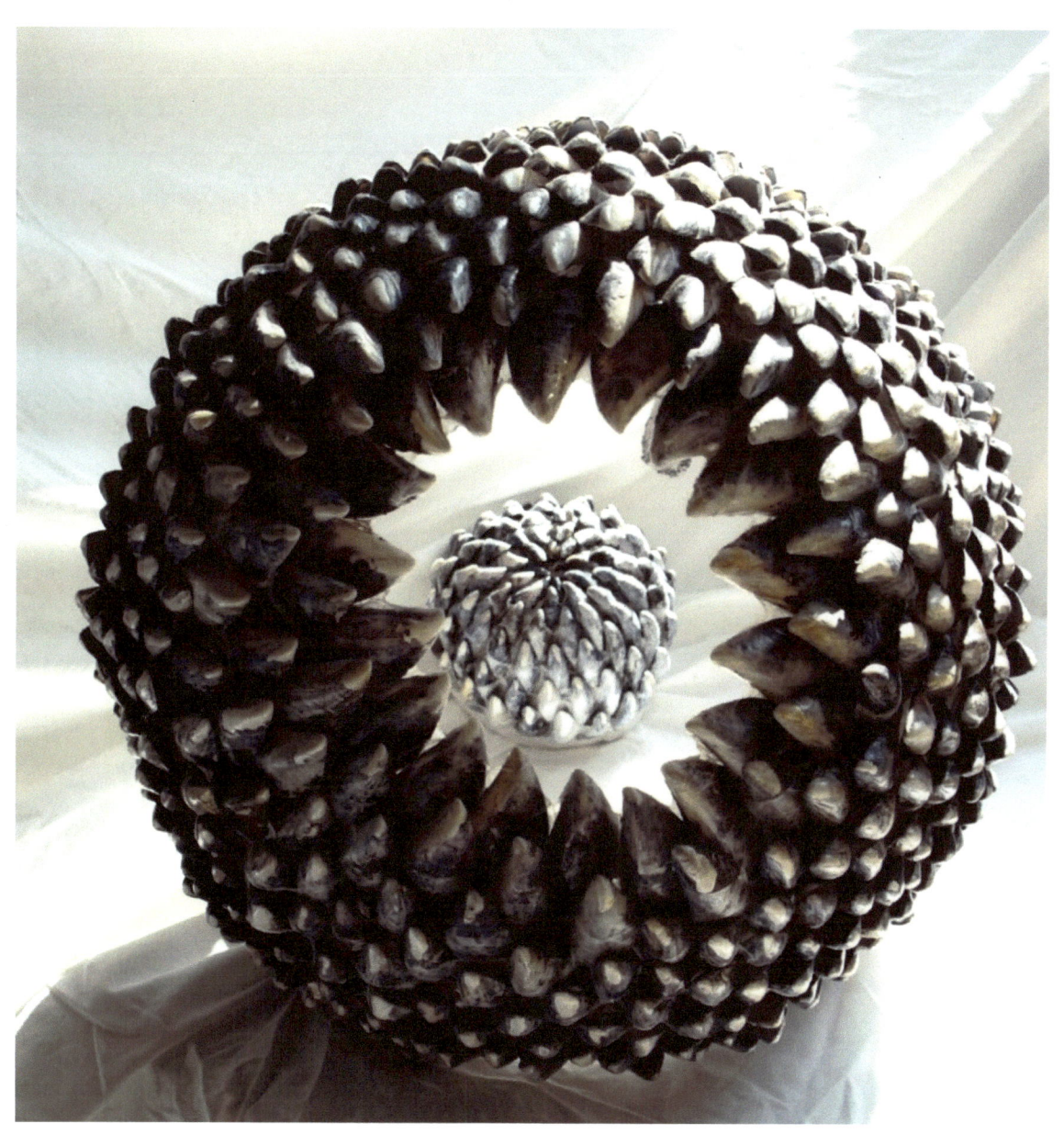

Opposite : Arial view of part of the installation.

Whilst creating the cone and some of the other pieces I crushed many shells to explore texture .

I discovered that they are surprisingly sharp !

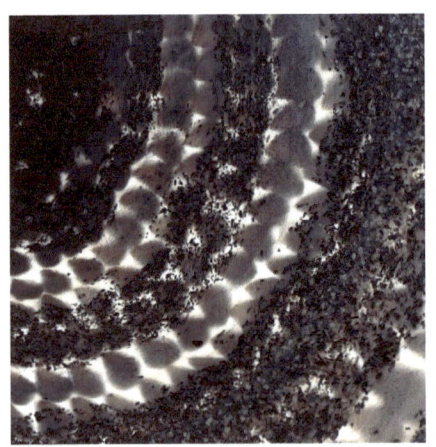
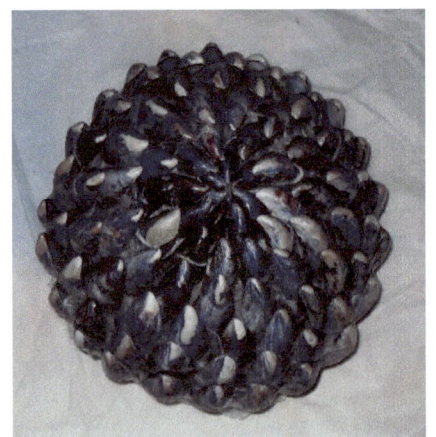
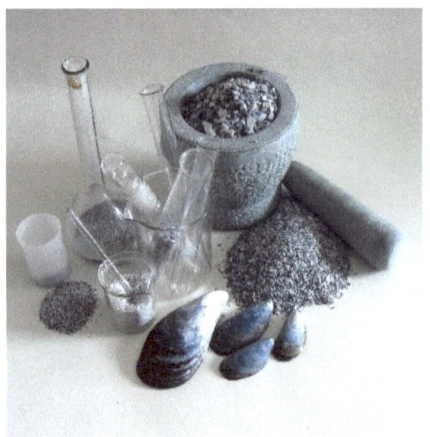

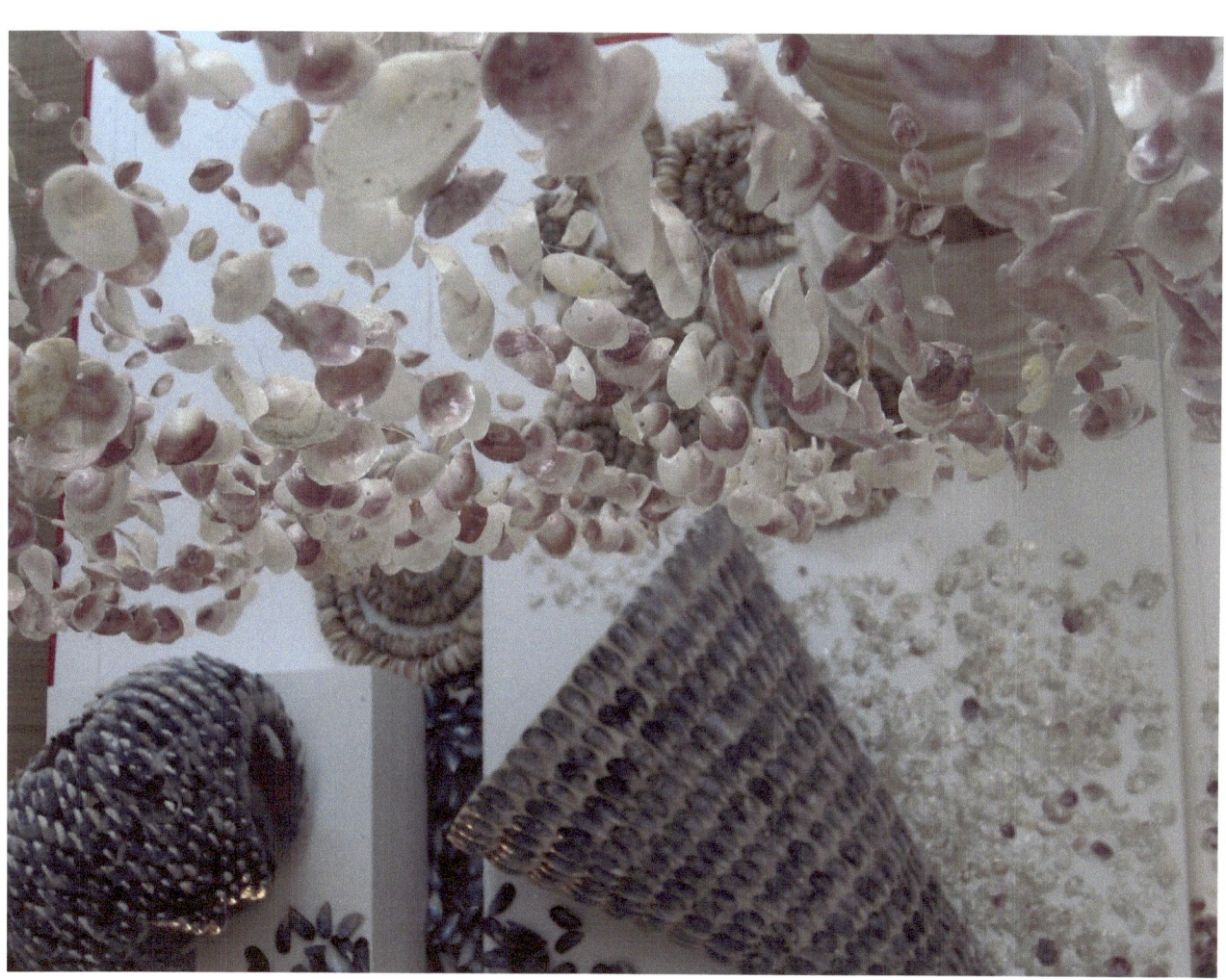

Limpets.

I only collected the ones with holes in. It's amazing how strong they are.

Did you know that the tensile strength of their teeth is the strongest biological material known? I didn't even know they had teeth!

I often admire the patterns they leave behind on their travels.

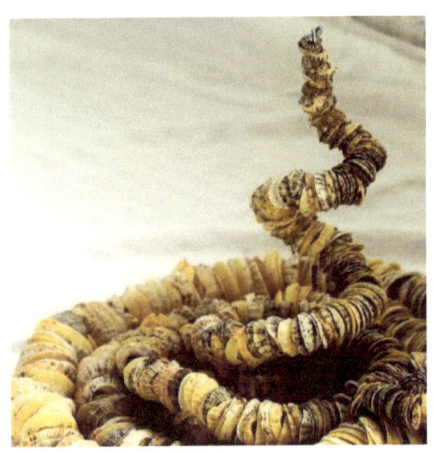 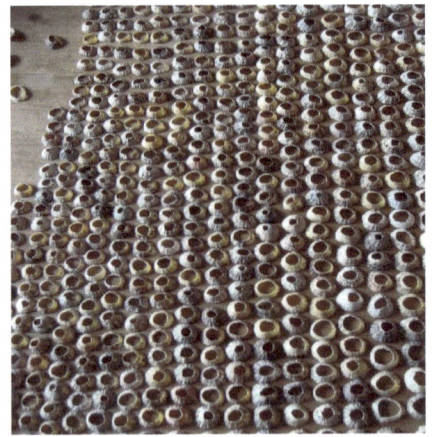 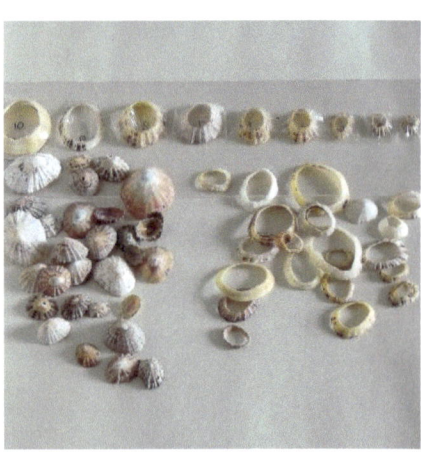

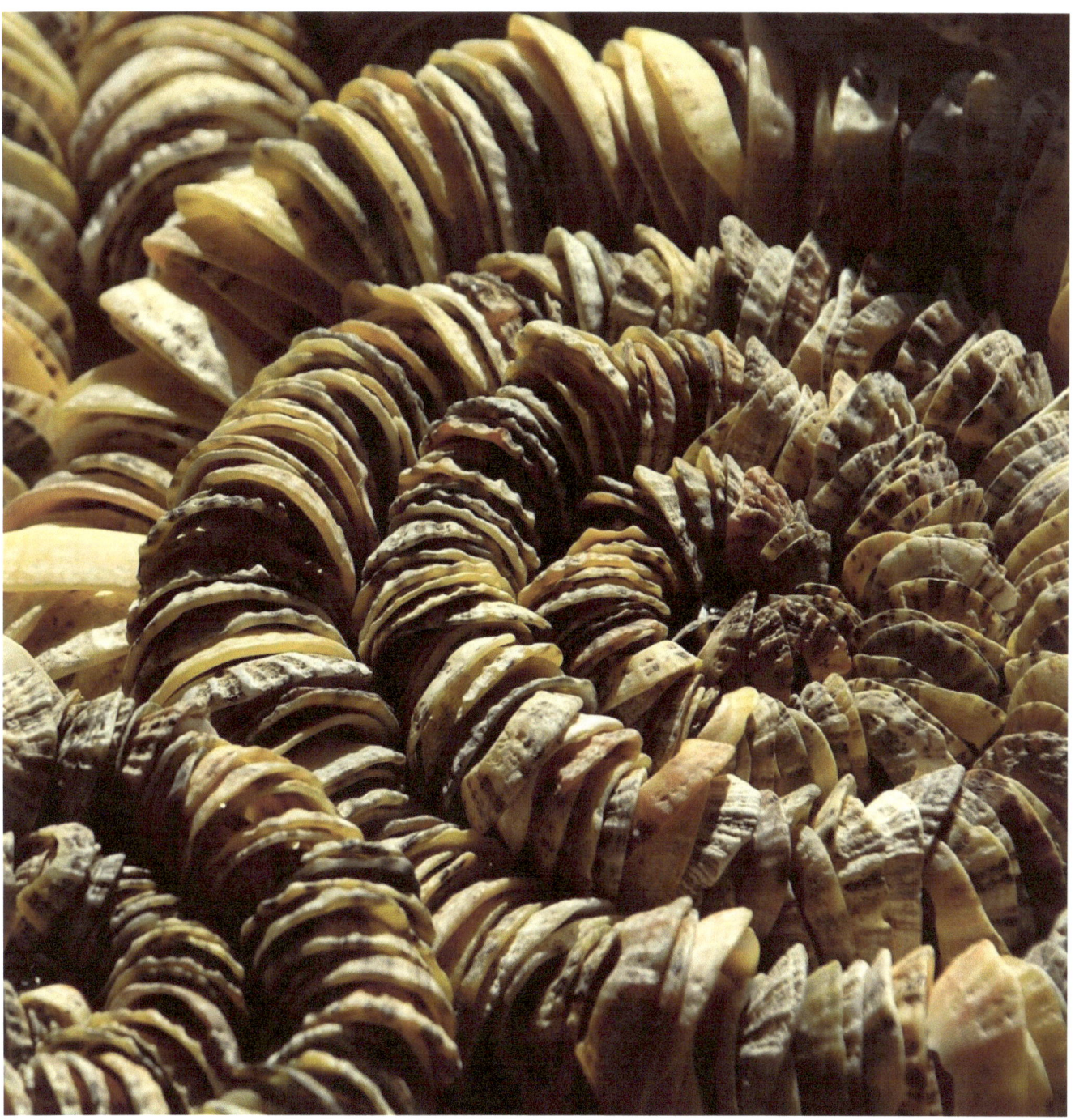

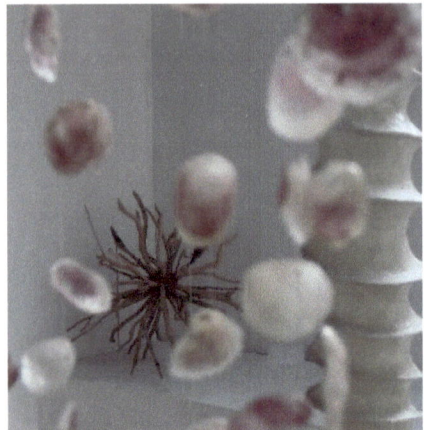

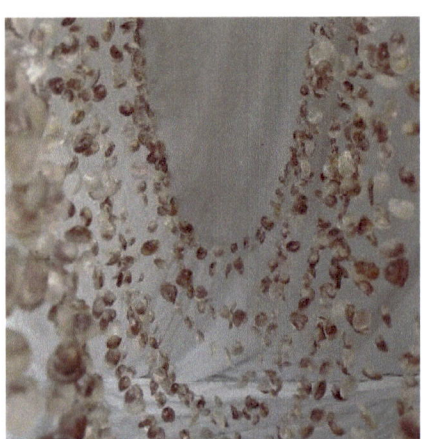

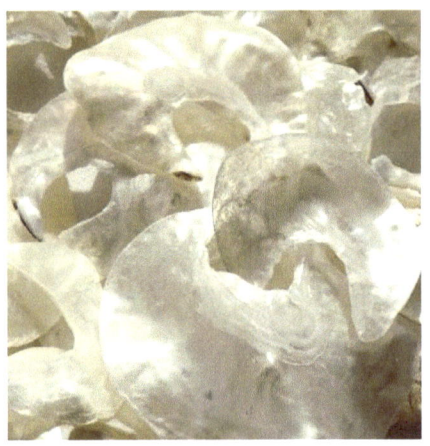

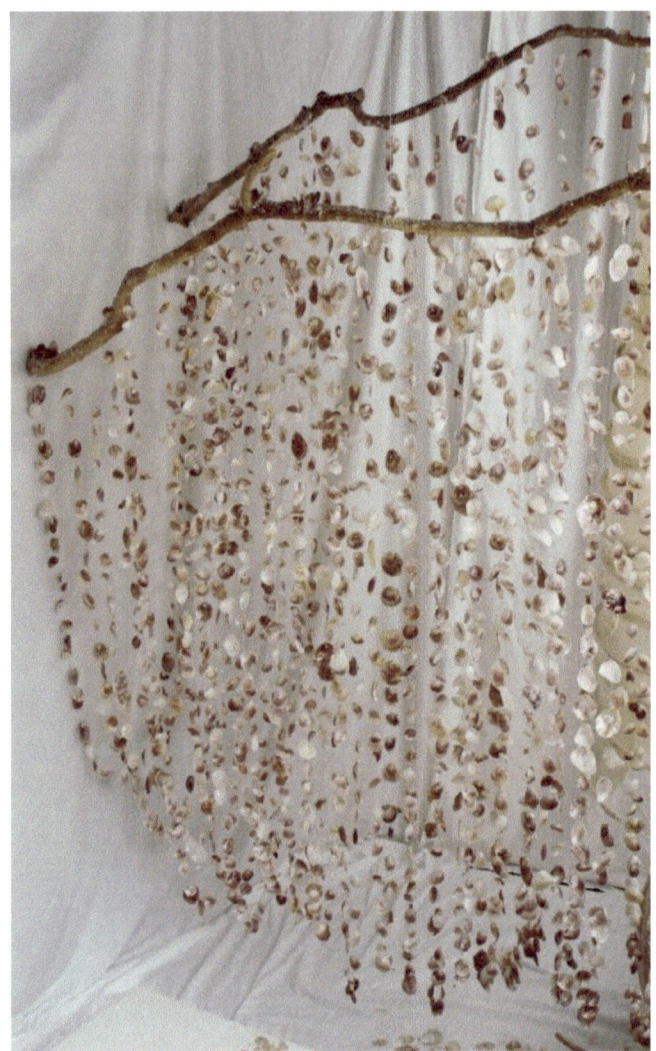

You can't miss the Saddle Oyster shells they are so bright, and they sparkle in the wet sand. Sometimes called jingle shells the jingling although delicate and lovely along the water's edge did drive me to distraction whilst I threaded hundreds of them onto fishing twine in my studio.

I saved the bottom parts for a later piece.

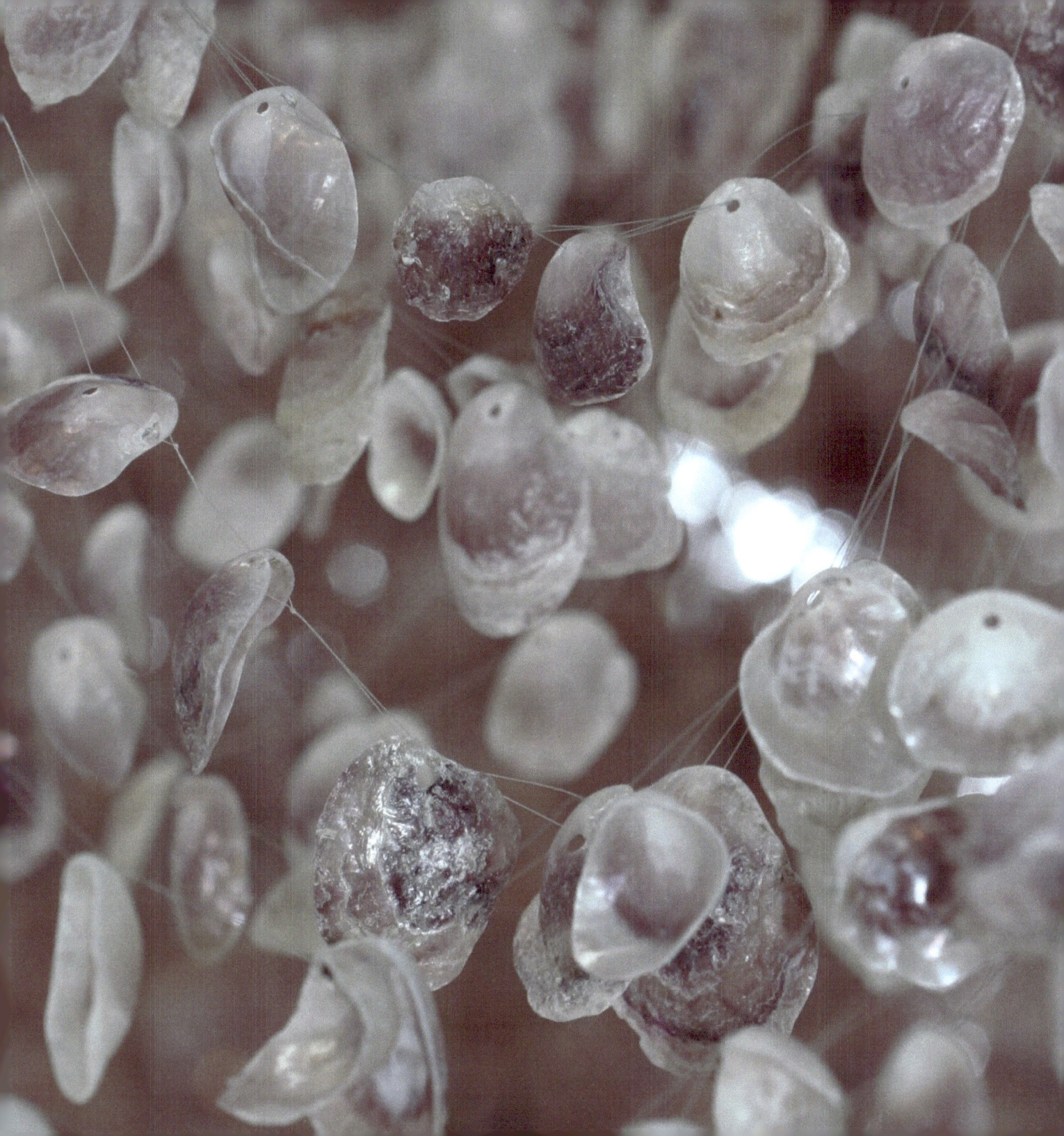

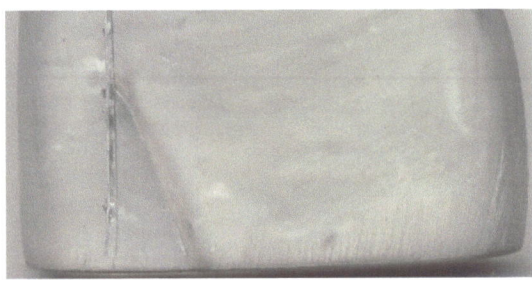

So ... I started playing with the scanner.

Experimenting with this tiny left-over piece of resin I came up with this beautiful image.

Besides myself with the possibilities I scanned a few things to within an inch of their lives.

Not that I had any evidence of these items being alive at the time nor can I say with any certainty that the said objects were not harmed during the process.

The next page shows the image of the fishbone I brought back earlier. I encased it in resin to suggest a fossil in crystal and after scanning I inverted the colours.

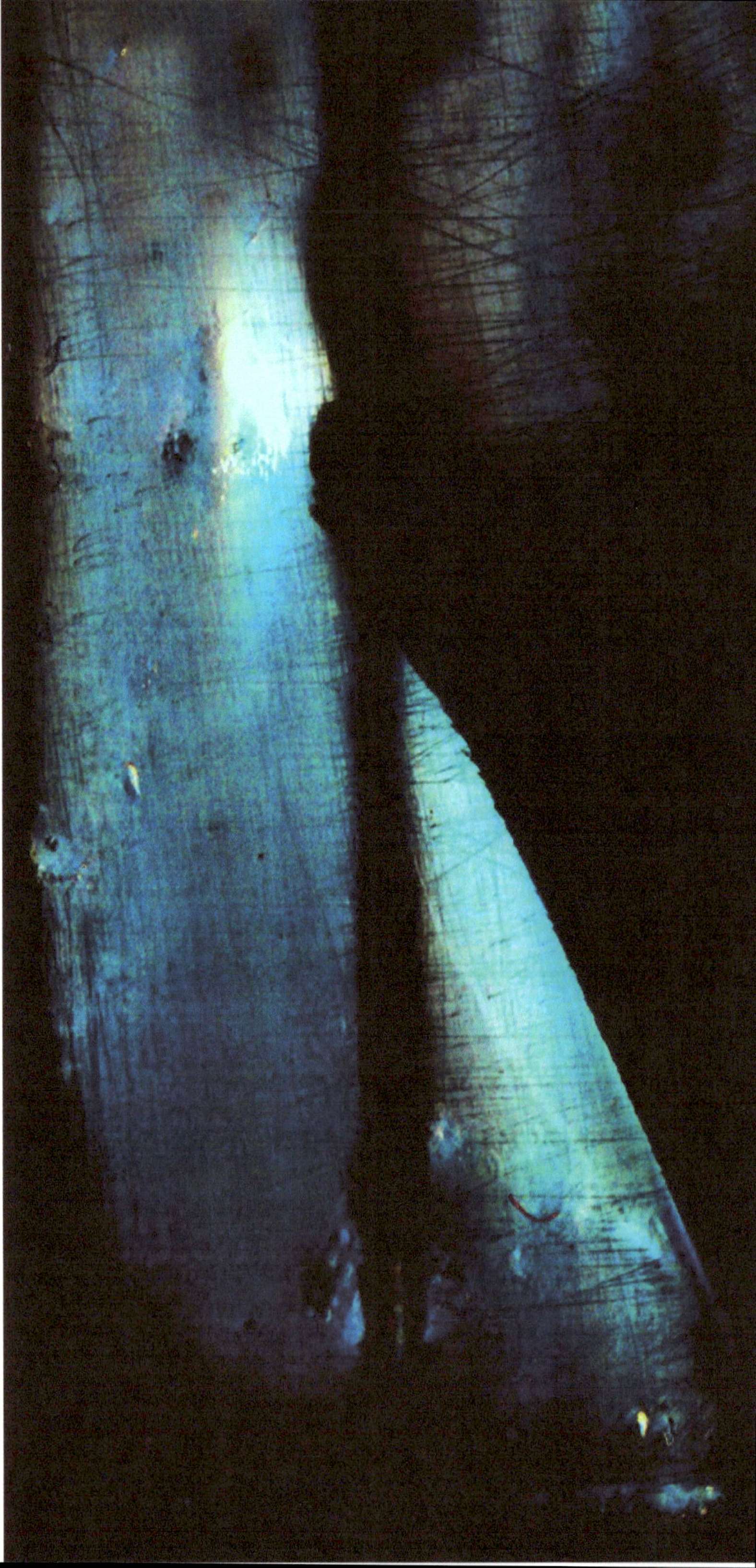

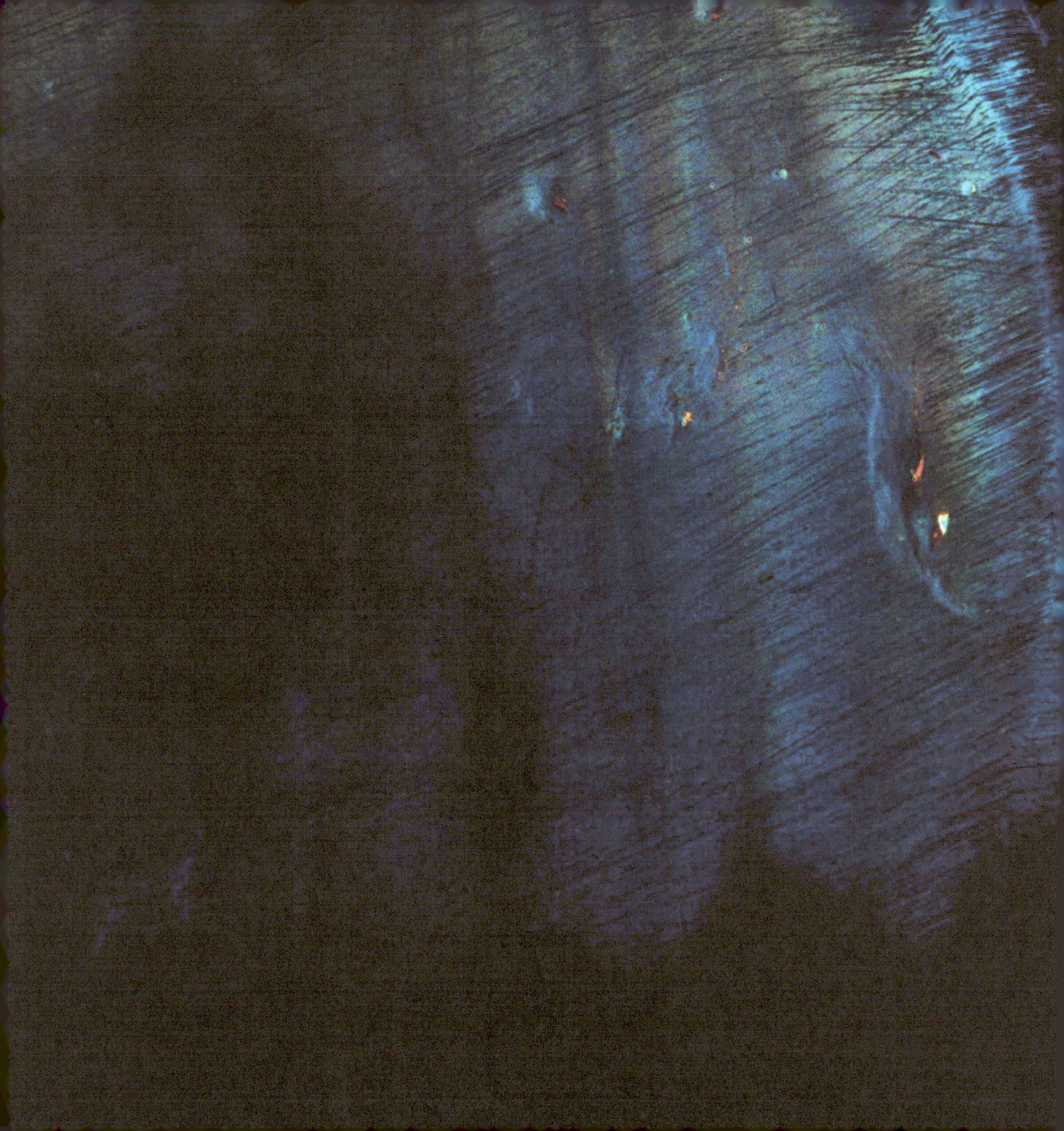

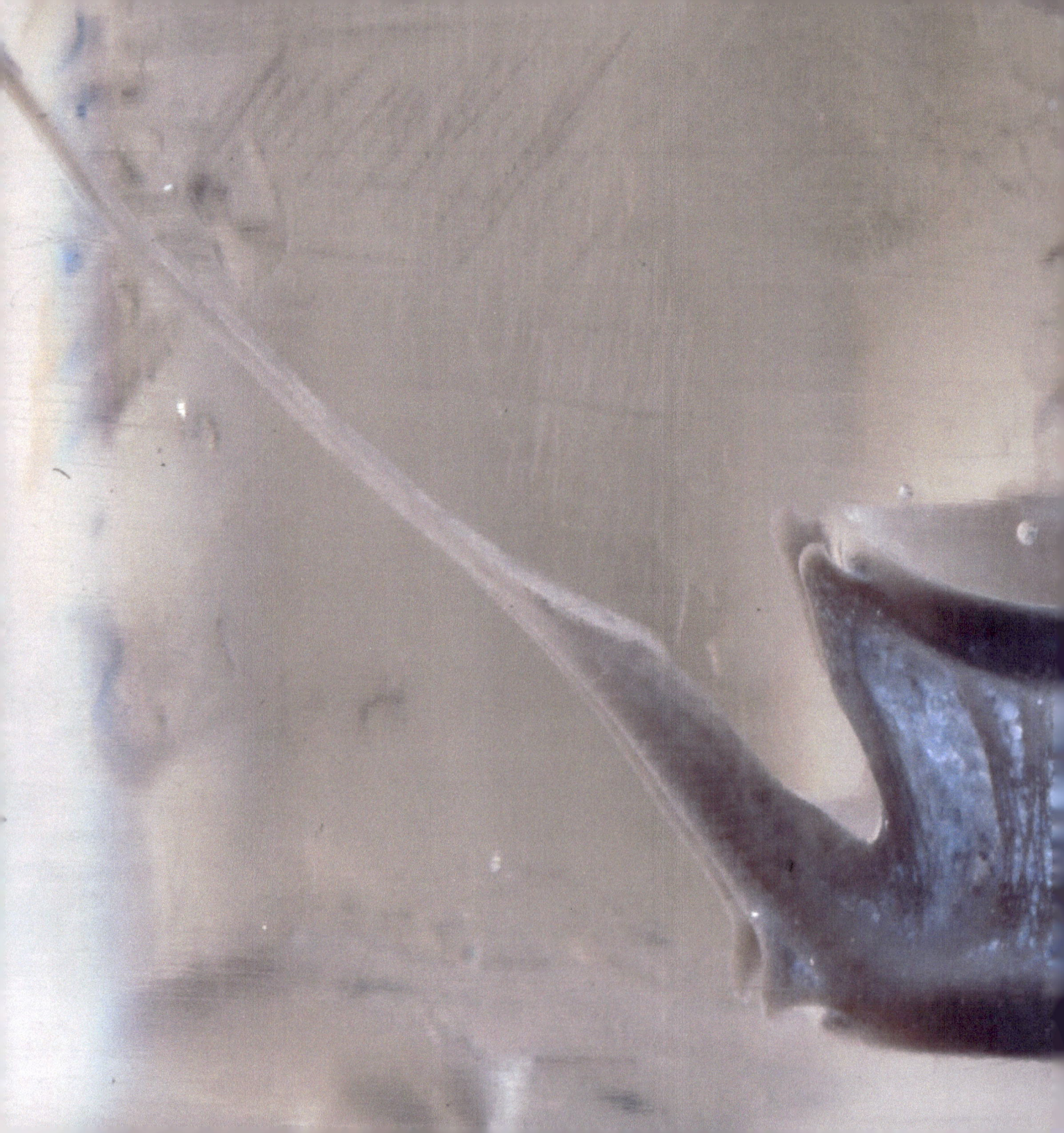

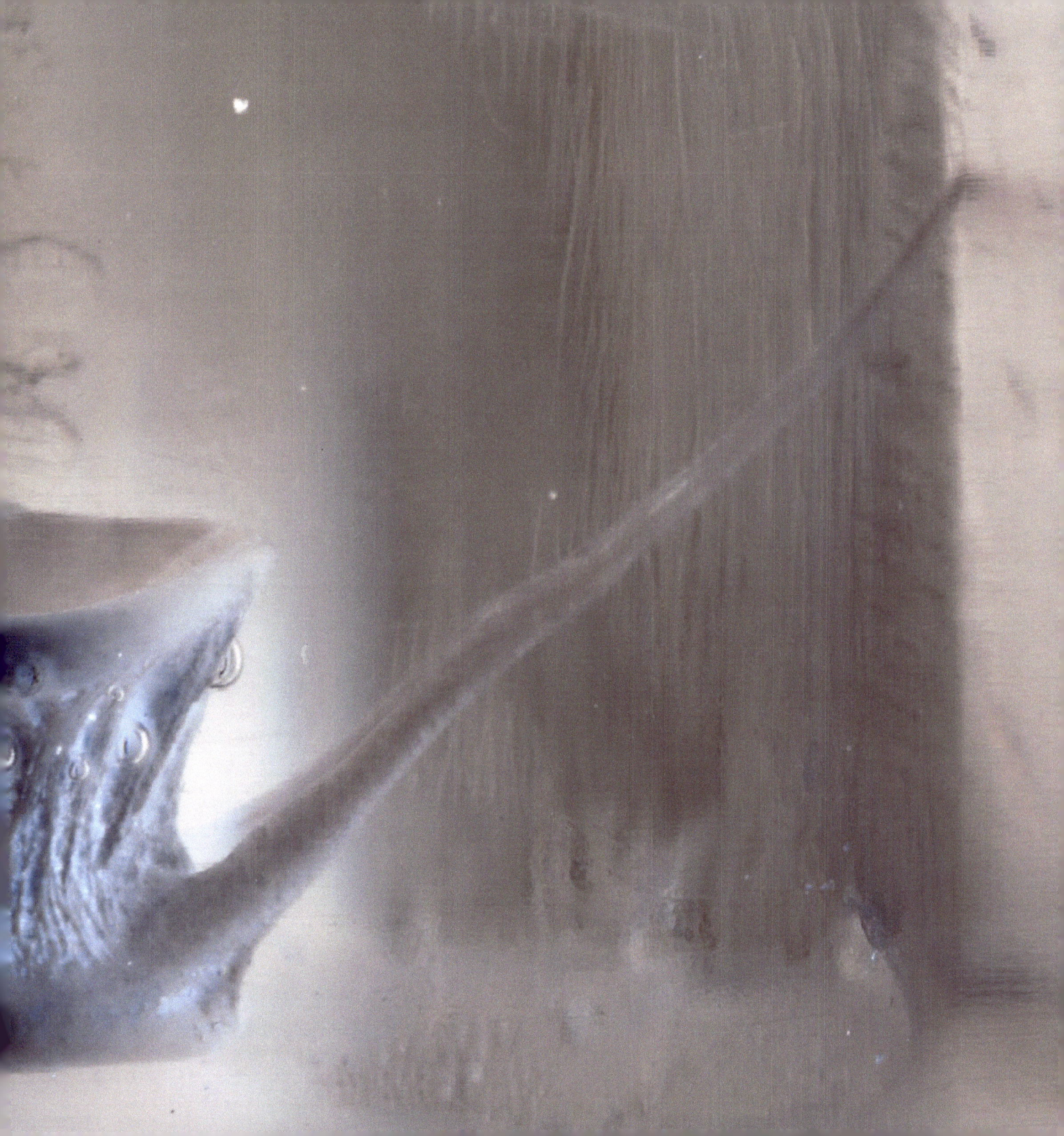

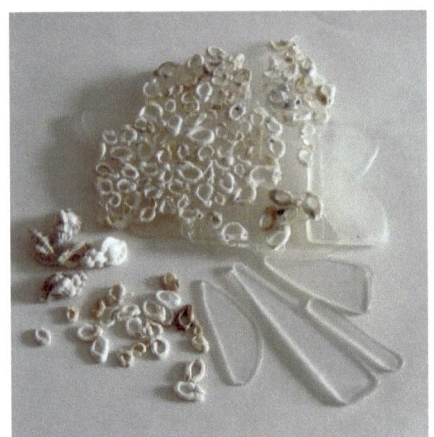
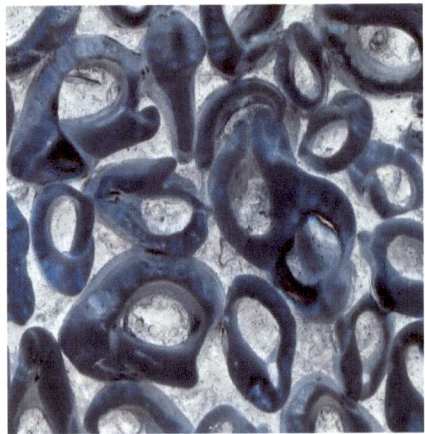
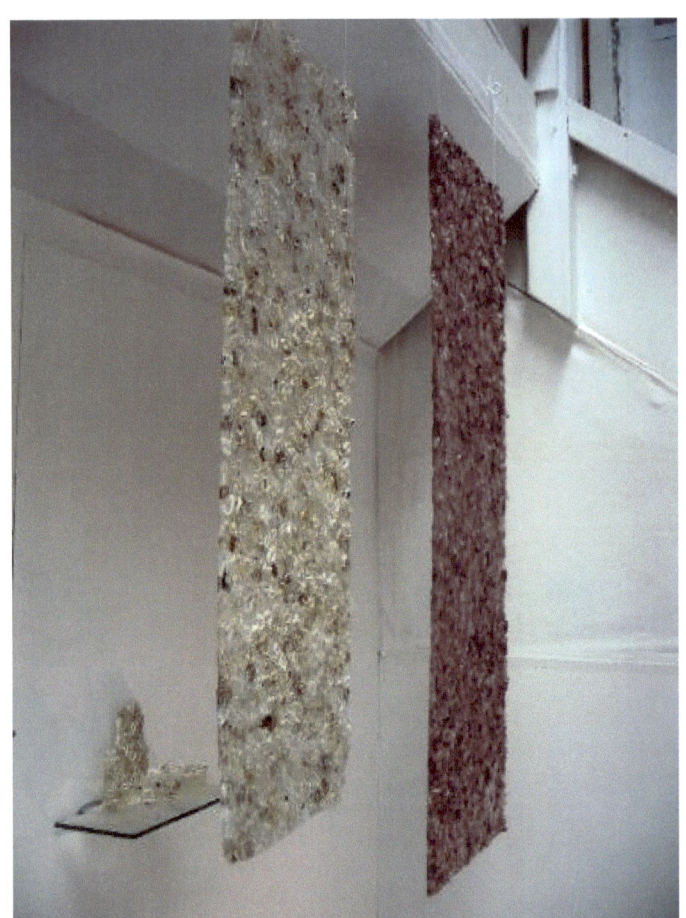

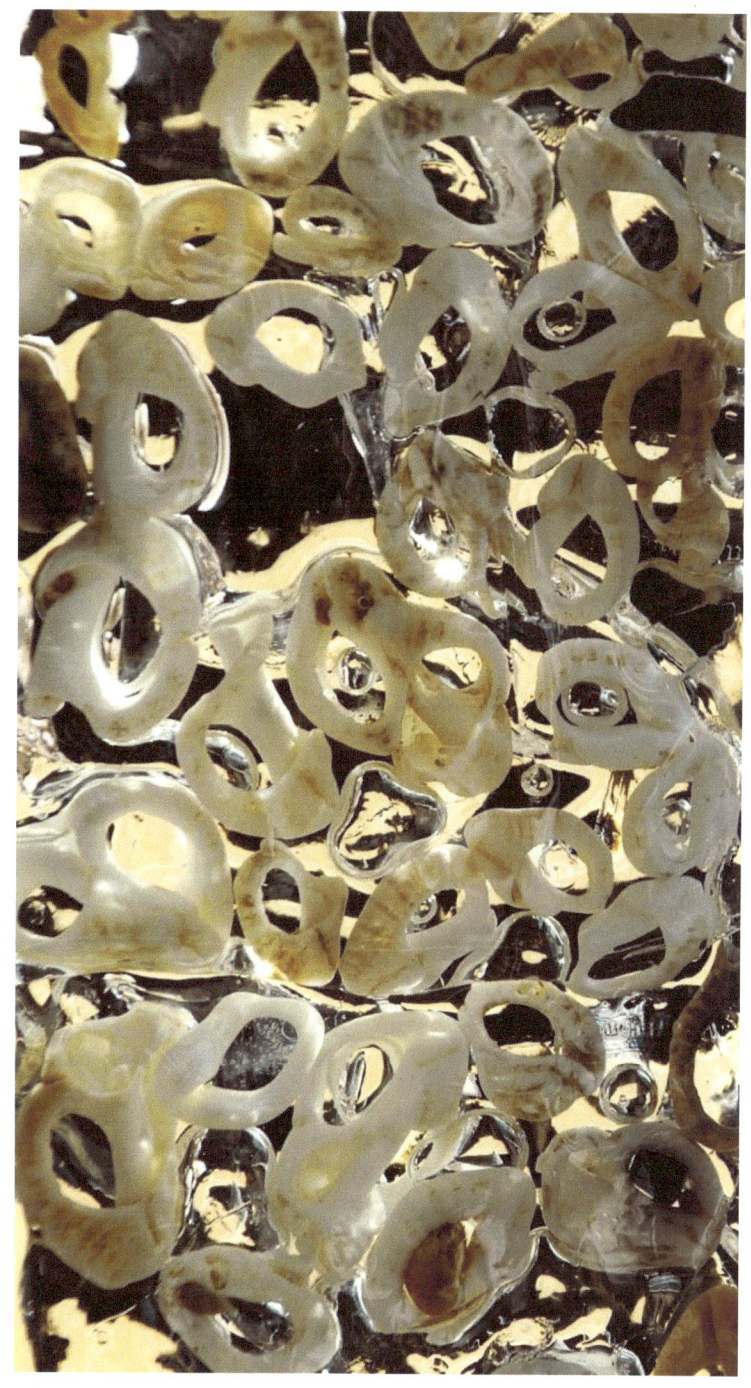

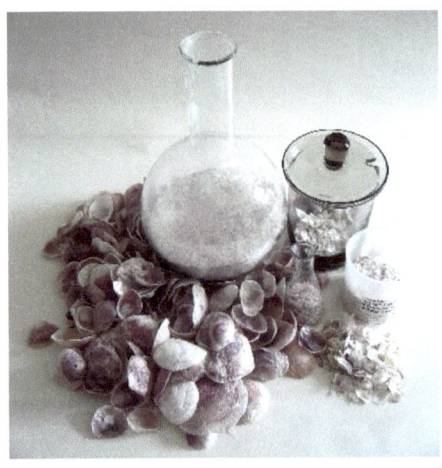

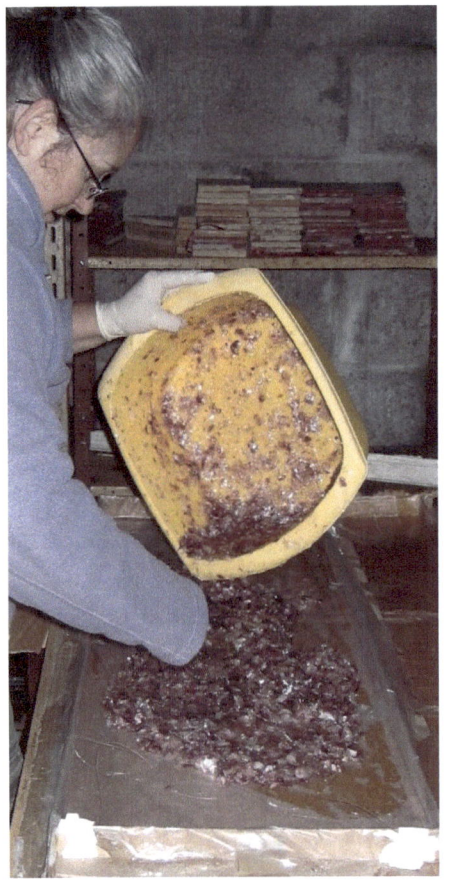

Embedding the crushed shells in resin was exasperating and smelly

I even managed to get some in my hair.

In the end it was worth all my efforts as the piece looked beautiful against the window as the light filtered through it .

My friend let my use her shed as my neighbours complained about the smell.

I did apologise!

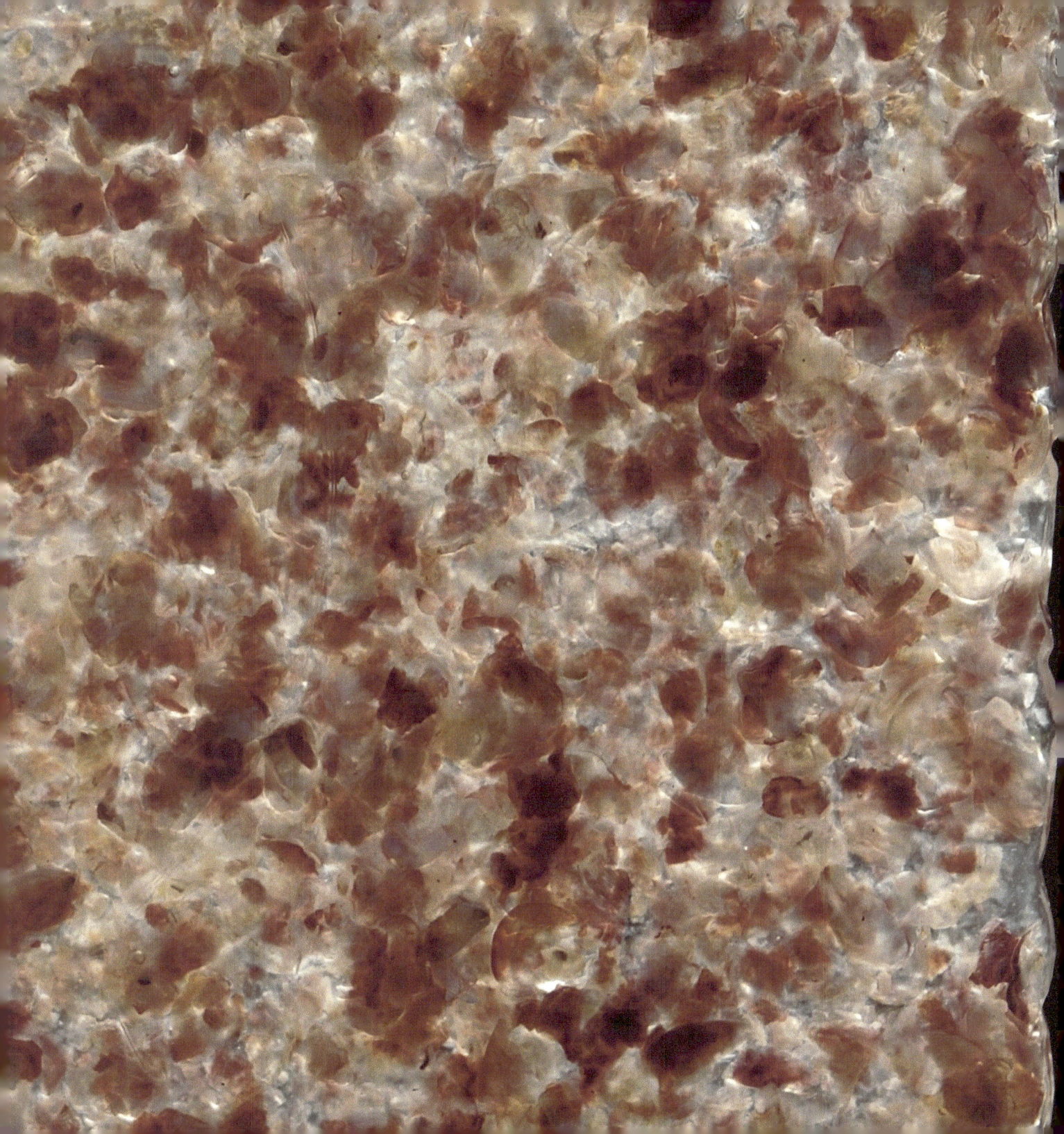

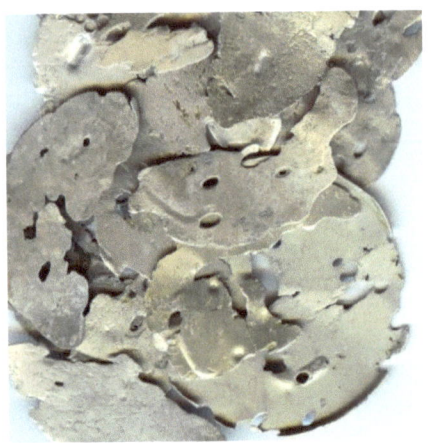
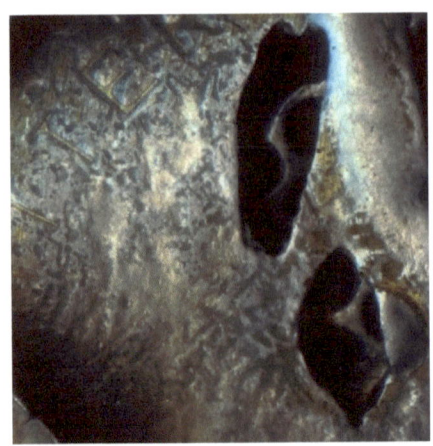

I definitely got besotted with the scanner -I even scanned a beetle at one point – don't think it liked it though and in any event the image did come out a bit skew whiff. It just would not stay still so I put it back in the garden.

If you haven't already guessed what these are...they are small metal bits mainly drink can tops that had been eroded by the tide.

Below I balanced as many as I could on a discarded metal comb and spring that I had found earlier.

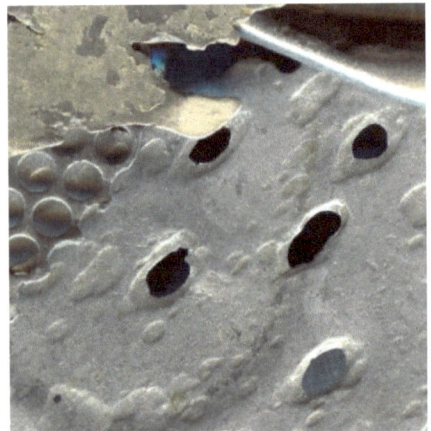
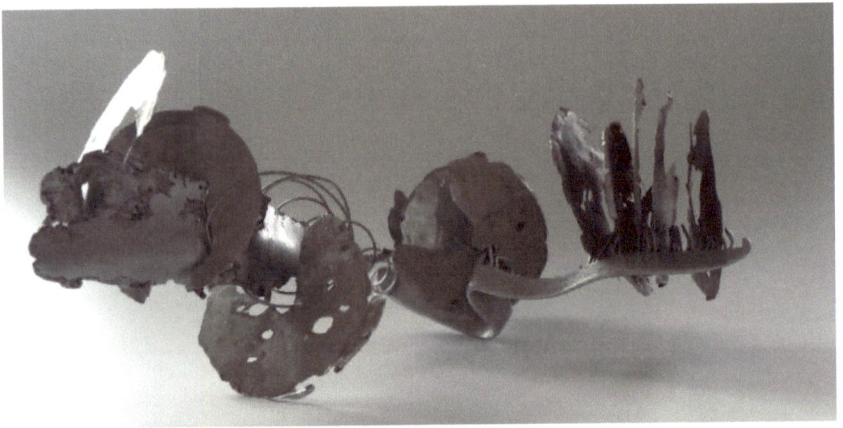
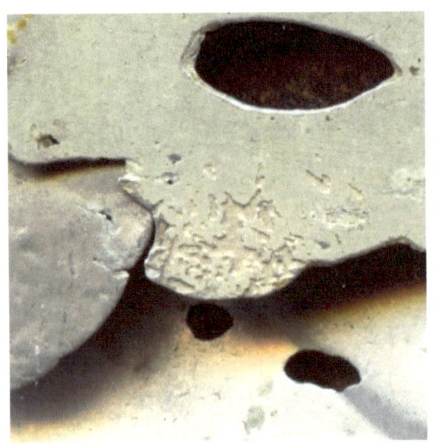

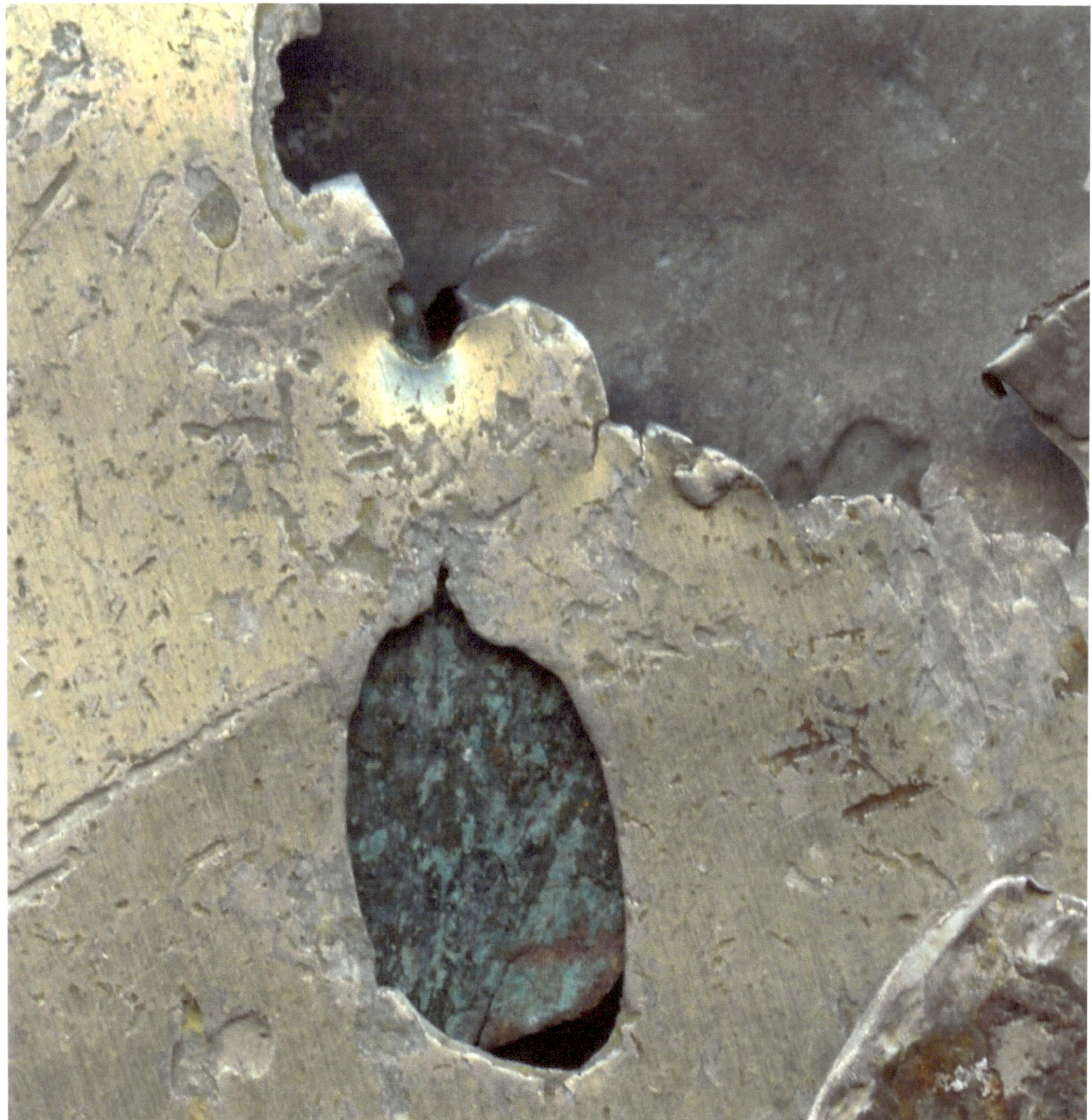

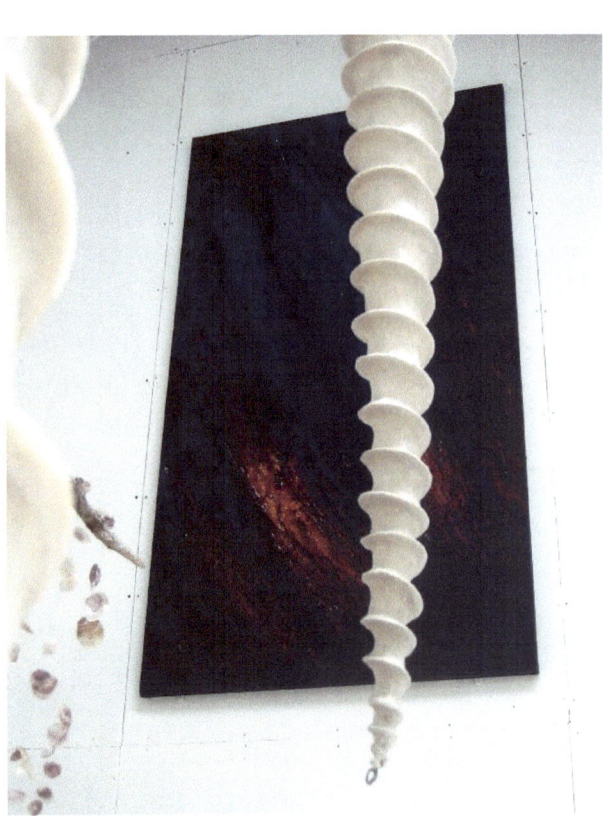

Acrylic on canvas 4 ft x 8 ft

I have been painting for ever, well it feels like forever - around 40 years.

I love colour.

My latest odyssey is working in layers. the more time that passes there seems to be more layers.

I often re work canvases when they are wet or dry leaving some of the under painting.

It is difficult to see the detail properly here in this tiny photo. Over the page gives you an idea of the texture and the brightness that bursts through what seems like a dark painting. There are many more colours than might first appear.

I was trying to show the power of the sun as it disappears into the night.

I spend a lot of time thinking about the universe and how I am connected to it, so for this project I decided to celebrate a tiny point in the cosmos our moon.

It has always fascinated me, besides its luminescence which is captivating to say the least, I am comforted by it being there.

My plan was to create something during each of the thirteen full moons that occur over one year but the project expanded into several.

I explore many art forms and can be found traversing the various beaches here in Devon. Incidentally any beach trip is usually accompanied by an irresistible urge to dip into the sea.

Down End Nr Croyde . North Devon.
My outdoor studio.

If you want to know more about me or my work visit my web site:

www.brendajet.com

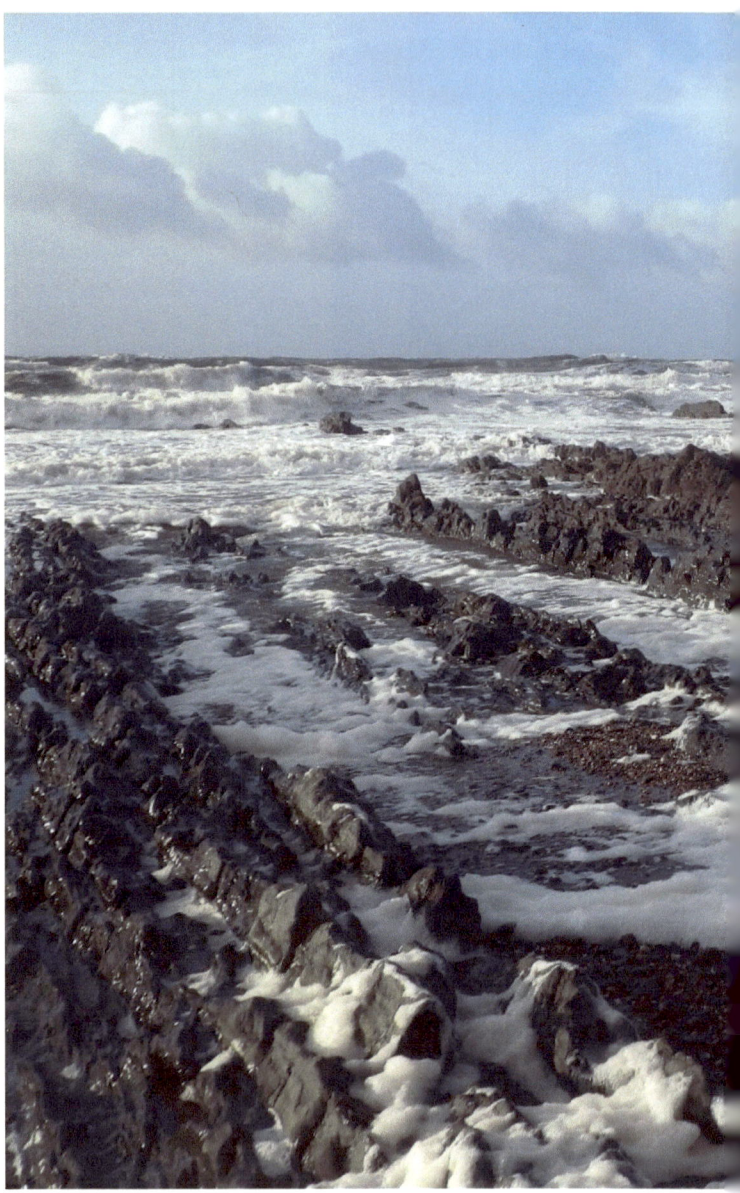

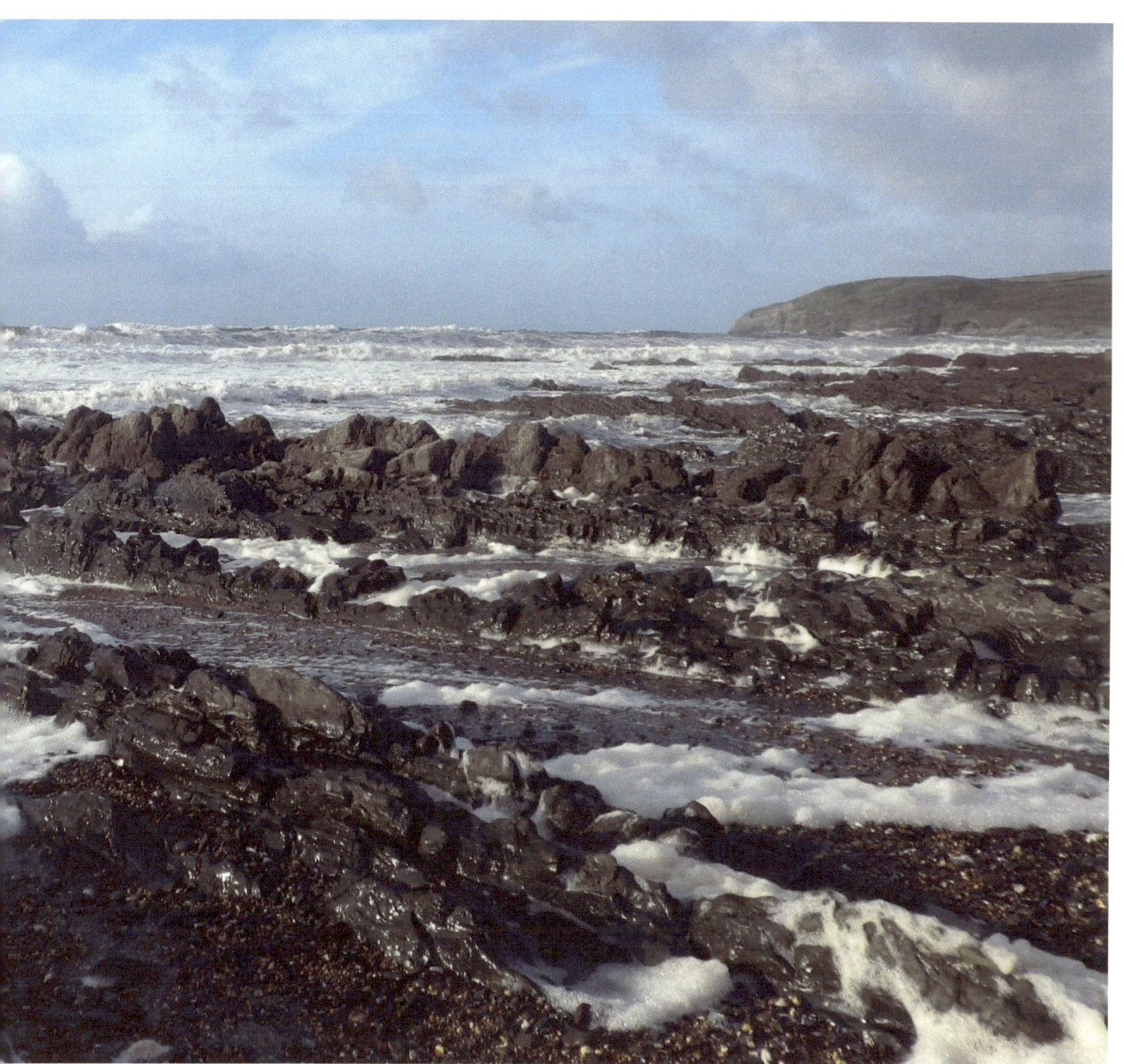

www.ingramcontent.com/pod-product-compliance
Lightning Source LLC
Chambersburg PA
CBHW042323250526
R18347300001B/R183473PG45473CBX00027B/29